Sensational

Living with a Sixth Sense

Sensational

Living with a Sixth Sense

Reflections on the development of a life
from emptiness and futility
to fulfilment and purpose

by Joan Lougheed

Sensational

Living with a Sixth Sense

Disclosure

These are all true extrasensory or spiritual experiences of mine as I have journeyed through life. Similar events that people have told me about over the years are shared here, and I trust, with their approval.

Names and places are all correct, however names of some tangential folk I have not been sure of, so guessed. They will however be able to recognise themselves as the accounts are affirmative and accurate as told to me or as I remember them.

The names of my children are their birth names, not the names changed at adoption.

The names of some organisations have, for clarity, been translated from their Afrikaans designation to their English equivalents.

* * *

"Write the vision, and make it plain upon tablets, that they may run that read it."

(Habakkuk 2:2)

* * *

And so, I offer it to you and pray that you may be inspired, blessed, and motivated as I have been.

♫ To God be the glory,
great things he has done. ♫

Sensational

Living With a Sixth Sense
by Joan Lougheed

Table of Contents

Preface

I and many others have had encounters with angels, the spirits of deceased people, and 'near death' or out-of-body's incidents, and so I share with you my experiences and those that people have told me about.

I know that all these events were neither figments of my or their imaginations nor flights of fancy as there is something breath-takingly awesome and life changing about each of these incidents. In some way in the recounting of such events, the teller finds difficulty in telling it or cannot find words to describe them adequately because they are 'other worldly'. While normal every day happenings tend to fade over time and become fuzzy, these otherworldly events are clearly remembered, even decades later.

Another clear indication for me of their authenticity is that the happening is not how I or they would have constructed them in our imagination but unconventional or outlandish, yet strangely perfect. All have been serendipitous or life-changing experiences to a greater or lesser degree.

It was only after my conversion that my spiritual senses were awakened, and I was able to distinguish spiritual from secular experiences. Before that, I could possibly have experienced paranormal events as coincidences or simply as 'feelings' without associating them with the extrasensory, paranormal spirit realm.

I also confess that prior to my conversion I had no church background, religious experience, Bible knowledge or interest. I thought of myself then as fluctuating between atheism and agnosticism.

As an atheist I did not believe in the presence of God here and now. In my thinking, if there had in the distant past been a God, then after creating the world he programmed it to run along on its own under human control. I thought of God as a fanciful being or 'comfort blanket' for those people who drew solace from that fantasy, or that their devotional practices were simply based on ritualistic habits and traditions.

As an agnostic, I reasoned that if there were a God in the remoteness of the heavens, he was unapproachable. If he connected with people, it would only be with those who were saints, religious fanatics, or devout worshippers, otherwise he would ignore the secular-minded, disinterested, or wicked of the world. Nonspiritual people I saw as simply living temporally, having no existence before conception or life after death.

With my spiritual awakening I now perceive that all of creation is under God's loving control and guidance. The difference between people and the rest of creation is that we humans are given the freedom to accept or reject God's influence on our lives.

And so, my story begins in darkness and chaos, and unfolds into glorious light.

* * *

Eye hath not seen,
nor ear heard,
neither have entered into the human heart,
the things which God hath prepared
for them that love him.

(1 Corinthians 2:9)

Chapter 1
Earthly Foundations

From an essentially worldly upbringing, my perception of a spiritual dimension to life was based on superstition, pious pretence, or false hope. Any acknowledgement of God was based on the ritualistic practices observed by my parents as learned traditionally from their strict religious upbringing in Holland. After both launched out into independence, my father to America and my mother to Britain, they eventually met in Canada, married, and settled in South Africa, adopting the British culture, but their spiritual sensitivity was superficial and practiced according to their Dutch family traditions.

My father was brought up in a strictly Christian home which meant obligatory church attendance on Sundays. Work of any kind was forbidden, which meant that sewing, mending, tidying, and homework had to be completed on a Saturday, leaving Sundays restricted to devotional exercise. Reading only of the Bible was permitted. Devotional practices during the week were grace before meals, thanks after meals and a Bible reading after dinner.

From my mother's upbringing, she instilled in us a religious awe, infusing a fear of causing offence in the spirit realm. Casual language with the mention of heaven, hell, use of the name of God or any spiritual utterance except in prayer, was regarded as blasphemous, wickedly profane and would bring down the wrath of God upon the offender. As a teenager I would on occasions put that to the test, standing at the window I would mutter, 'Bloody Hell,' or 'Goddamn it,' and hold my breath waiting for the onslaught. There followed no lightning strike, nor was the sun darkened. The birds kept singing and the sun shone brightly, so I concluded that either there was no God, or He did not care about me or what I said or did.

For me, religion was archaic, irrelevant, or belonged to an alien realm. I sensed that it was superficial for both my parents as Church attendance was dropped after my eldest sister fainted in church and, having been embarrassed thereby, refused to go again so, as we always did things together as a family, we no longer attended church. Thereafter Sunday became a day of family recreation. My father did however continue the practice of saying grace before and thanks after meals, in High Dutch. We were required to seal the prayers by reverently muttering 'Amen'. After dinner, the large, tattered *'Der Kinder Bybel'* (Children's Bible) which was the grandparent's gift on the birth of their first grandchild, was brought out and a story was read aloud by my father. When he got through to the last story in the book, he would begin again the next night with the story of creation. This was the traditional practice in my parent's religious upbringing, so they continued faithfully in retaining the ritual.

We were expected to repeat the last word or phrase of each Bible story, to prove that we had been listening attentively. It was easy for us to let our minds wonder, but as soon as Dad stopped speaking, the attention would leap back, and the last word recalled and repeated, to prove that we had been paying attention. With my rebellious nature in my late teens, I would deliberately mispronounce the last word and my father probably realised that these ritualistic practices, all in High Dutch, were wasted on me. And to me, this religious gabble in Hollands expressed to me that if God existed, he was a foreigner and I neither spoke his language nor he mine. So, I grew up having nothing to do with a foreign God.

I grew up then, with no interest in God. Why should I? Even my own grandparents were strangers to me. I never met them, and they never communicated with us, their English-speaking grandchildren.

South Africa was a multi-lingual country but governed then by the descendants of British or Dutch settlers. The white population were thus either English or Afrikaans speaking. My father having been well travelled, decided that English was the universal language, so English was our home language, and we children were sent to English schools. The uncles, aunts and cousins having emigrated from Holland, spoke High Dutch at home and went to Afrikaans schools.

We all understood Hollands as it was spoken when the uncles and aunts got together, but it was fun for us children to pretend that we did not understand them so we could follow adult conversation and their jokes.

* * *

Train up a child in the way he should go:
and when he is old, he will not depart from it.

(Proverb 22:6)

Chapter 2
Hints of an Invisible Realm

During my growing years I occasionally became aware of the fleeting presence of spirits of departed human beings. The home that we lived in from around 1942 to 1960, when I was aged two to twenty, was visited by a male ghost. Perhaps 'visited' is the wrong word, for we sensed that it was his home while he was on earth, and he simply came home from time to time. We were the squatters in his house, but he graciously accepted that. My two elder sisters and I sensed his presence on occasions, but my mother and brother never perceived his aura. I am not sure if my father sensed him or not as he never denied or admitted to it. Later in life and in other places I occasionally became aware of a spirit or the soul of a departed human being making their presence known. I will tell of those experiences later.

Betty, nine years my senior, sensed and saw our ghost, as he manifested mainly in her bedroom. She would tell us that she often saw him sitting in the corner of her room while she was doing her homework, but that he did not bother her. He was a friendly spirit, that of a young man in naval uniform. On a couple of occasions when the parents were out on one of their bridge evenings, Betty out on a date and Junior at scouts, Clara, and I alone at home and quietly reading or chatting in the lounge, would sometimes hear our sailor's footsteps walking down the passage from Betty's room, then stop in the doorway to the lounge. After pausing there he would disappear. We never saw him though, just heard sounds of measured treads.

Other than the spirits of departed souls, I had no awareness of angelic beings. Angels appeared on Christmas cards or were mentioned in children's prayers. So, I grew up with a sense of the presence of an invisible realm, but my beliefs hovered between atheism and agnosticism as far as heaven was concerned while coping with living in the material world.

Junior, four years my senior and involved with cubs and scouts, joined the Methodist Sunday School with his scouting troop. One day when I was about twelve, he came home and coaxed me to come with him to Sunday school. The lure he used to persuade me was that there was to be a Sunday School picnic a few weeks away and those were great fun, with games and sailing on the lake, hot-dogs for lunch with ice-cream to follow and an enormous urn of Ginger beer on tap. The added incentive was the promise of a prize-giving at the end of the year with book prizes for all; the size of the book dependent on regularity of attendance. I learned later that his class gained merit points for enrolling a friend or sibling.

The picnic was as much fun as promised and at the end of the year I received a book, although I had only begun attending Sunday school a few months before. The prize giving and end of year party was the last time that I attended Sunday school, as I had a humiliating experience and vowed that I would not go back there again.

What happened was that instead of lessons our class had a quiz. A box with strips of paper with a simple or challenging question on each was passed around and each pupil dipped in and randomly chose one, then read it out and if she knew the answer, she was given five points. If she got it wrong, she would lose a point. If she did not know the answer the person with the lowest total score was permitted to answer and gain a point. When my turn came to read my question out, which was 'What did God create?' I did not know the answer. All hands shot up and a babble of, "Oh, that's easy! Please Miss, I can answer that," reverberated around the class.

The teacher, sensing my embarrassment and being helpful said to me. "You'll find the answer in the very first sentence in the Bible." She handed me her Bible and I opened it, paged through to the first page. I looked through the first sentence, but I couldn't find the word 'create' there, nor in the second or third sentences. "Read it out," said the teacher.

So, I read aloud: "This Bible is the English translation as authorised by his majesty King James of Great Britain and preserves the living Word of God." A roar of laughter swelled around the class and the rest of the Sunday School turned in their seats to see the cause of hilarity. I was mortified and somehow sat through the remainder of the morning, but on my way home I vowed never to return.

When I got home, I placed my book prize on the bookshelf and took down my library book. Religion was not for me. The family did not question me not going back to Sunday School when it reopened after Christmas. Junior did not go back either as he had graduated from the senior class and did not join the evening Confirmation Class.

My sisters and I grew up with no church affiliation and when the time came for each of us, in turn, to be married, it had of course, to be in a church as at that time it was customary to marry in church. Betty got married in the church of her future sister-in-law as her fiancé was not religious either. She married without the fancy trappings of wedding dress, or bridesmaids. The reception was a barbecue with friends and family in the garden.

Clara's fiancé was a non-practicing Roman Catholic, so she was married in the Catholic church, but it was not conducted in the sanctuary, but in the lobby of the church on Sunday morning after the congregation had left.

My fiancé's family were Dutch Reformed, though only Martin's father attended church regularly. The future parents-in-law insisted that as I had no church affiliation, we marry in their church. We agreed, but I insisted that it had to be the most beautiful Dutch Reformed Church in that village, so we drove around looking for the prettiest church. We noted the phone number on the board outside the church and phoned to book an appointment with the dominee. He asked our business and then informed us that, as we were not members of *that* church, we were to approach the minister of the church of my fiancé's parents.

A week later we met with the dominee in his rectory study to discuss the wedding service. I was astonished at the number of little children popping into his study to show Pappa their pictures, receive a cuddle and a sweetie from the jar on his desk. I wondered how this 'holy man' had managed to have so many children. Was God only a God of the daytime or in the church building on Sundays? Or did Dominee Prinsloo and his wife switch God off at night when they switched out the lights? Perhaps God could not see in the dark.

Furthermore, despite my request, the Dominee insisted that he would *not* conduct the ceremony in English as the DRC was an Afrikaans Church. He told me that if I wanted the ceremony in English then we would have to go to the Methodist, Presbyterian, or Anglican Churches down the road. Having been loosely connection with the Methodist Sunday School as a twelve-year-old and as Martin was amenable, we considered approaching the Methodist minister, but Martin's mother insisted that, as I was not churched and her son was at least confirmed in the DRC, we comply with their wishes. So, we were married in the Dutch Reformed Church. Neither of us entered a church again for the next ten years.

When our elder son, Tony was four, we decided, for several reasons, to send him to Sunday School. The logical reason was that he would be going to Nursery School the following year, so we thought that he needed to be introduced to a classroom type environment, one morning a week for a start. Secondly, he was a handful, and I desperately needed a break, even for only an hour a week. Most importantly, we were doing our best to give him a good physical and emotional foundation and intended providing the best education to develop his intellectual ability, and for him to develop fully, a spiritual grounding needed to be provided. In which religion could God be found if there were such a Being? We would start with the Christian faith and then work through all the other religions to enable him to discover for himself in which religion he would be satisfied. Furthermore, it would please the paternal grandparents.

To set a good example I decided to start going to church. I enrolled him into the Methodist Sunday School and bought a hat. On the first day we settled Tony into Sunday School then went across to the church, only to discovered that the Church Service was an hour later. Ah, well, home again, but walking down the hill we saw that the doors to the Roman Catholic Church across the road were open and people going in. Well, I had the hat, so I said, "Let's go in there."

"No! My parents would be upset if we went to the Catholic Church," said Martin.
"Why? What's the difference?"
"I don't know. You go if you want to. I'm not going," was his reply.

So, I went across the road and joined the crowd going in. When I got to the door, I noticed that each person paused to dip their fingers into a bowl of liquid (probably water) and touching their faces with the wet fingers, turned, curtsied, and did whatever else was expected of them. No, I did not understand the rituals and realised that church was alien territory to me so rather than make a fool of myself again or make a mistake and offend someone I had better go home. Indeed, church was not for me.

Tony however enjoyed Sunday School and loved to sing the songs that he learned there. One Easter weekend, we went for a drive, and sitting in the back of the car, he began to sing mournfully:

"Low in the grave he lay,
Jesus, my Saviour,
waiting the coming day,
Jesus, my Lord:"

I was horrified at the woeful songs they were teaching little children in Sunday School. Then suddenly the tempo changed and with a whoop he began belting out the chorus:

"Up from the grave he arose,
with a mighty triumph o'er his foes;
He arose a victor from the dark domain,
and he lives forever with his saints to reign:
He arose! He arose!
Alleluia! Christ arose!"

Wow...! I was startled by the enthusiasm of his joyous and triumphal singing. The impact it had on me remained for a very long time.

A few months later Tony came home with an invitation to a tea party, extended to all the mothers of children in the Beginner's Department, to meet the teachers. I accepted the invitation with enthusiasm as I saw this to be my first exposure to parents & teachers meetings.

As I entered the hall a young woman at the door welcomed me, asked my name, and displayed delight at meeting me, telling me what a wonderful and intelligent little boy Tony was. She then told me that she was thrilled at having him in her class. Of course, that warmed me to her immediately. She hastened to get me a cup of tea and took me across to the table laden with a vast selection of cakes and tempting savoury snacks. We chatted a while and then one of the older women asked us all to take our tea and cake through to the adjoining hall and to sit at one of the tables set up there.

In the larger hall several small tables were covered with pretty tablecloths, a bowl of sweets and a vase of fresh flowers in the centre. There were four chairs around each table and in front of each chair a sheet of paper and a pencil. Lynn, the young woman who had met me at the door, took me to the table nearest the door and sat down beside me. Two other young women joined us, greeting us warmly and introduced themselves. There was a wonderful friendly atmosphere that I had never experienced before.

The older woman who had asked us to come through to the main hall welcomed us all again and introduced herself as Connie Pedersen, the wife of the minister and told us about her interests and her four teenage children: three boys and a girl. She added that

21

God gave us our children when they were adorable tiny babies so that we could learn to love them before they became teenagers. To my surprise, she came across as a quite ordinary wife and mother and not as a pious, holy untouchable. I liked her.

She asked us to chat amongst ourselves and while we chatted to take time to fill out the questionnaire before us as she and some of the teachers had thought that if we enjoyed this morning, we may like to do it again or on a regular basis. If so, to write down what we would like to do. We filled out the forms individually with our particulars and discussed with one another what our interests were and what we would like to do if this were to become a regular event. Connie came around to each table to chat with us and collect our completed feedback forms. She then closed the meeting with a short prayer, bade us a safe journey home and said that she would let us know what the decision would be as gleaned from our feedback forms.

I enjoyed that afternoon immensely. Meeting in a friendly group with other young mothers filled a vacuum in my life that I had not been aware of until that morning. Having moved away from family and friends in Johannesburg, down to Cape Town three years earlier, I had felt deprived of social contact with women of my age. These young women were the nicest people that I had ever met. I certainly would like to do that again, and regularly.

A couple of weeks later I received a letter in the post telling me of the outcome of the parent/teachers meeting and stating that all of those who attended the party indicated that they would certainly like to do it on a regular basis. Most of the ladies indicated that we should meet fortnightly and at the same time and on the same day, but that we ought to break for the school holidays.

The group who had originally planned that meeting had drawn up a programme for the following term as the school holidays were approaching. The schedule was enclosed in the letter. I read through it and was delighted to see that in that twelve-week cycle, there would be only one devotional talk, and that by a missionary from Kenya. The other weeks included a flower arranging class; a talk from the Meat Board about different cuts of meat and suggested recipes; making pictures using dry flowers; a cake decorating demonstration; a visit by a child psychologist... I was certainly looking forward to joining the fortnightly meetings.

It was to be known as Young Mother's Fellowship, and we were assured that it would be quite separate from the Women's Auxiliary constitution.

* * *

....and a little child shall lead them.
(Isaiah 11:6)

Chapter 3
Awesome Auras

The Young Mother's Fellowship turned out to herald several transforming experiences in my life. I had noticed at the initial gathering that this group of young mothers of the children in the Beginner's Department of the Methodist Sunday School and their teachers were different from any young women of my acquaintance. I simply could not put my finger on it. Yes, they were friendly, but so were my friends; they were helpful and caring, but so were my sisters. But there was an aura of otherness about them all that I couldn't place and had never encountered before, except perhaps in my next door neighbour, Liz.

Liz was what I would call a nice person. She was always happy and self-confident. A positive person in the extreme that somehow made me feel a little uncomfortable, like the time I complained to her about that dreadful woman across the road, Mrs. Van Schalkwyk. She never divulged her Christian name, so she was always Mrs. Van Schalkwyk, though she was in the same age bracket as Liz and me. Her youngest child, Lee, was the same age as my Tony and Liz's Linda.

24

Yes, Liz was different. I first realised it when telling her about something that Mrs van Schalkwyk, across the road, had done and said to me. Liz, rather than being shocked, simply said, "Poor woman. She must be awfully unhappy. Perhaps she's lonely. Why don't you invite her over for a cup of tea?" Well, I did but got the brushoff.

Another time I popped over to Liz to return the cup of sugar that I had borrowed that morning, but I did not get further than her front door. There were some cars in her driveway. She had visitors, but no matter, I was not going to stay, only hand over the cup of sugar. I raised my hand to ring the front doorbell and paused as I heard them singing. They were singing *hymns*, of all things! Although I wasn't a church goer, I did recognise *hymn* singing. We had sung hymns in school assembly way back when I was a schoolgirl, and in my brief sojourn at Sunday school as a twelve-year-old. I scampered off back home. I would return the sugar tomorrow.

Although I was painfully shy and felt different from all the other young mothers, I really enjoyed the YMF meetings. Well, I did not much enjoy standing around and chatting as I really had nothing in common with these women, except that we all had a child in the Beginners Department of Sunday School or taught there. But talking about our children was exhausted at the pilot gathering.

We started with tea and cake as members arrived and stood around chatting, then we would go through to the main hall for the activity, lecture, or demonstration. I would usually get there early as I hated making a grand entry. I would slip in quietly, pick up my cup of tea then go to the library in the corner and browse through the books. One of the other young mothers would usually come and join me and we would chatter about whatever she wanted to talk about, hopefully nothing that would drag me out of my comfort zone.

There was one young mother that I tried to avoid. The first time Ina cornered me she asked, "Are you saved?" I hadn't a clue what she meant by that. I had not been drowning, although I felt as though I was in deep water or something worse. At the next meeting she came across to me and pressed a little booklet into my hand saying, "Take that home with you and read through it and we'll talk about it next time." The title of the booklet was 'The Four Spiritual Laws'. I left it on top of the piano when her back was turned. Thereafter I casually made a beeline for the other side of the room when I saw her approaching and she fortunately got waylaid enroute.

I did borrow a few books from the YMF Library. I had told Gillian about a book that I had taken out from the local Library and found fascinating. It was by Erich von Daniken called 'Chariots of the Gods?' She was a little sceptical and said, "Try that," and handed me 'Prison to Praise' from the YMF Library. It was indeed interesting, as were the others that I occasionally took out, but they were all religious books, and I was not by nature religious. I wished I was. I was at that time more interested in discovering who I was, where I had come from and where I was going. I could not see a connection with the spirit realm or that God would be interested in me. I felt that I would have needed to be born into a religious family. Too late for that.

There were a couple of talks that made quite an impact on me. One was a visit from a missionary from Malawi who had been sent out there by the Methodist Church. I had not been looking forward to that meeting as I much preferred the secular activities and did not much enjoy those with a religious focus, which I termed as brainwashing.

Ah well, here I am so I would listen and let it wash over me. Joan Judd was, as all of them, one of those especially nice people. They all seemed to love her and were buzzing around her like bees around the queen bee. She was not in the least bit physically attractive; quite plain in fact, wearing no makeup, her hair not styled nor was she smartly dressed. She was, what one would probably call a typical missionary. She talked about her work and experiences in the mission field. All that washed over my head, but there was something magnetic about her that strangely drew me.

As she spoke, she glowed. It was as though she was enfolded in an aura of light. I wondered if that was what artists who painted pictures of saints and angels with haloes saw. As she spoke, she appeared to be drawing inspiration from a Being of light/power/Love – and she glowed! That light/love/power radiated from her.

There is a God! She knows Him... and He loves her!' My heart raced with the revelation and my yearning soul cried out, *'I want what she's got'.* I went home that morning in a daze, transformed from a cynical atheist to a craving agnostic.

* * *

"Call to me, and I will answer you,
and show you great and mighty things,
which will surprise you," says the Lord
(Jeremiah 33:3 NIV)

28

Chapter 4
The Strange Visitor

I do not know whether it was a week or several months that passed after the morning that I was struck by the vision of God's power and love flowing down as a beam of enlightenment to inspire Joan Judd as she shared with us her experiences as a missionary, but that vision certainly created within my soul a spiritual thirst.

Another and more subjective event took place at the last meeting of Young Mother's Fellowship that year. It was scheduled as an end of year party. I arrived early, as usual, and was surprised that Connie was waiting at the door to greet me. "We're first meeting in the church for a short service and Holy Communion, then we will come to the hall for our end of year Christmas Party," she said.

I was bewildered and disappointed, as a church service and Holy Communion were certainly not what I expected or wanted. I was ready to forgo the party and go home rather than that. "Sorry, I didn't realise we were to go into church," I said. "I haven't got a hat."

"We don't wear hats in church anymore. You are fine as you are," she said. "Come, I'll walk with you." So, she walked with me to the door of the church. There was no escape for me without embarrassment, which would have meant that I would not go back to YMF after the Christmas break — a repeat of the humiliation of my last day at Sunday School.

On entering the church, she said, "Please sit on the right-hand side and in front. People always tend to fill the back pews first, but there are so few of us this morning it'll be better if we sit in the front pews." So, I headed for the very first row of seats under the podium and sat down. I was the first one there.

I looked at the row of books in the rack in front of me. There was a slim brown one, a fat black one, a small chunky maroon one and a typed paper booklet. I didn't know which was the hymn book, which the Bible or what the other two were. With no one in front of me to observe, I wouldn't know which book to use if needed, and I was sure we would need to use one or other. Besides that, being unfamiliar with church and with worship practice, I wouldn't know when to stand, sit or kneel. I felt extremely uncomfortable. I wanted to disappear through a crack in the floorboards, but there was no escape now.

As the other YMF members came in they began to fill the seats behind me. "Oh, God, why did I have to sit in the front row? Please let someone come and sit here beside me so I can watch what she does," I prayed.

I had never, to my knowledge, done *that* before, except for the Lord's Prayer in School Assembly and rattling off the bedtime prayer under my mother's supervision:

'And-now-I-lay-me-down-to-sleep-I-ask-the-lord-my-soul-to-keep-if-I-should-die-before-I-wake-I-ask-the-lord-my-soul-to-take...God-bless-Mummy-Daddy-Betty-Clara-Junior-Joan-and-everybody-else-I-love. Amen!'

My plea that morning in the church was indeed a heartfelt prayer rather than a wish. After all, here I was inside a church so, I called on that God who knows and loves Joan Judd. Perhaps he will remember that I was there that day and will hear my desperate appeal.

I opened my eyes to see a young woman standing by the front row of seats waiting for me to let her through. I moved along to make a space for her to sit beside me. I didn't recognise her and realised that she must be a visitor or someone passing by and seeing an open church, came to the service. She did not speak to me but simply sat down, quite at home there and not behaving like a stranger at all. I noted that she too was not dressed for church. As a matter of fact, she projected serenity – so much so that I felt totally relaxed, at peace and strangely contented. I thought it strange that she should come to our closing session.

Because I knew that we are not supposed to talk in church, I decided that after the service I would follow her out and welcome her, explain that this was our closing meeting for the year, invite her to the party and see if she would like to join YMF.

The service began and she was totally familiar with the proceedings. Good! I watched which book she picked out as the hymn was announced and was impressed that she opened to the correct hymn number without paging through to find it. However, she followed but did not sing. Maybe she had lost her voice or was dumb. She certainly was not deaf.

The time came for Holy Communion. A cloth was taken off the paraphernalia on the table and again I felt a ripple of anxiety run through me. I had heard that one was not permitted to take communion if not confirmed, and I had not been confirmed, so what do I do? No one knew that I was not confirmed so should I go up anyway and follow what everyone else did? That would not be right or honest. Not in a church, anyway. Do I abstain and be exposed as an impostor, or do I do what everyone else was going to do and risk the consequences for dishonesty in this, God's abode? Being struck by lightning would be the easy way out but making a fool of myself by not knowing what to do or how to do it I could not live with. Besides that, I felt that it would not be right to dishonour this religious ritual by participating without understanding.

"Oh, God, I don't want to do the wrong thing. Let this visitor beside me guide me. I'll follow her example."

One of the members came alongside and gestured for us to go up to the railing in front of the table. The visitor made no move, so I too remained seated. Jenny and Barbara, who had come in late and had edged past us both to sit on the other side of me by the wall, shuffled past us now and smiled at me but, to my surprise, ignored the visitor. Not very friendly, I thought, but felt totally at peace within myself, sitting there as each group at the railing were served in turn. Then after a short prayer they returned to their seats. I was enjoying the atmosphere, soaking in the tranquillity that surrounded me.

The service ended. We all rose to make our way to the hall for tea. The visitor moved out in silence, weaving her way between the other women. No one greeted her. I tried to follow her but was blocked in by groups of YMF members chattering to each other. (I thought one was not supposed to chatter in church.) When I got outside, the visitor was nowhere to be seen. Had she gone straight to the hall for tea? I hurried down but she was not there. She may have been offended by the lack of hospitality shown her. I felt saddened and surprised. They were all always extremely friendly.

Over tea Connie came to me. "I don't want to embarrass you," she said, "but I noticed that you didn't go up for communion…"

"I've not been confirmed," I replied simply.

"Oh, that ruling is only for the children," she explained. "In the Methodist Church the Table of the Lord is open to all who love Jesus."

"I don't know him, how can I love him?" was my response.

"I see – fair enough. I only asked because you were the only one who didn't go up for Communion and I wondered why," she explained.

"I wasn't the only one," I replied. "The woman sitting beside me didn't go up either."

"There was no one sitting beside you," she said. "Do you mean Jenny and Barbara? They both went up."

"No… the young woman sitting next to me – to my left," I said.

"There was no one sitting next to you." she replied, looking puzzled. By now a group of young mothers had gathered around us looking mystified.

They looked at one another in bewilderment. "That's right," said Gillian. "I felt sorry for you sitting alone and thought that someone ought to go and sit with you, but then you looked contented on your own. Anyway, Jen & Barbara came in and sat up in the front pew along from you."

"But I wasn't on my own. The visitor came in and sat next to me," I insisted. "She must have been blocked from your view by those sitting behind us."

"There was no one sitting directly behind you," remarked Trudy. "Who was it?" she asked. "Where is she now?"

"I've never seen her before" I replied as I looked around the hall. "She's not here now. She must have gone home"

"What did she look like?" By now the little group were muttering among themselves and looking completely baffled.

So, I began to describe her to the bewildered group: "Short golden-blond hair, clear blue eyes, with a fine, radiant, almost translucent complexion. She was plain, but lovely. She wore a white short-sleeved blouse embroidered and buttoned down the front, with a Peter Pan collar. Her skirt was floral, in pastel shades, gathered at the waist, and she wore white sandals. She had no handbag with her," I added. 'That was strange' I thought to myself. 'She had no handbag, nor pocket for

35

handkerchief or car keys. I wonder how she got here or had gone so quickly. Had someone picked her up? I had not noticed a car driving off as I got out of church shortly after her.

I was beginning to feel embarrassed with all the attention. I hoped that she would come again so that these women would not think that I had lied, gone mad or been hallucinating. But I never saw her again.

A few months later I did however discover who she was and was overjoyed when I realised why she had come to that service on that day.

* * *

Are not angels ministering spirits sent to serve those who will inherit salvation?

(Hebrews 1:14)

Chapter 5
Preparing the Way

The Young Mother's Fellowship recommenced after the schools reopened in January. The gatherings unfolded and were as stimulating as before. We learned how to make pictures from dried flowers mounted on panels of balsawood. Being artistic I excelled in that. It was great for my self-esteem to outshine the rest of the group in something, at least. We also made corsages from sweets rather than flowers.

I was delighted to learn much from the talk by the meat board on different cuts of meat and how best to prepare them. I had never been a good cook and remember shortly after we married, I was looking forward to preparing my favourite stew, remembering the delicious and succulent stews my mother made.

On the way home from work, I bought a large oxtail from the butcher and put it on to simmer with the accompanying vegetables that I remembered from my mother's stews. Potatoes, carrots, an onion, a couple of bay leaves, a sprinkling of thyme, parsley, and a pinch of salt, all brought together to simmer for about twenty minutes while I set the table and prepared a desert for the evening meal. Half an hour later I lifted the lid of the pot, pricked the potato and carrot. The meat was nicely browned, so I thickened the juices with gravy granules, and we sat down to enjoy the meal.

What a disappointment. It was nothing like the succulent stews my mother always made. The meat was as tough as old leather boots, and we could not eat it.

Growing up at home, I had never learned to cook as my father had not welcomed what he called children's cookery experiments. He insisted that cooking, shopping, and housework were my mother's responsibilities. She kept house and served basic family meals, producing nothing exotic or imaginative, only wholesome dishes for us to enjoy.

One of the sessions at YMF was what was called 'Tempting Tasties' and we were asked to bring a favourite savoury or sweet dish for us each to sample. The accompanying recipes from each member were collected and compiled into the YMF Recipe Book, which I still use to this day, fifty-five years later, but not the recipes that I had submitted at the time as they were all handed down from my mother. She tended to substitute peanuts for pecan nuts in her nutty biscuits and cocoa, butter, and sugar for chocolate in her chocolate mousse, as well as other economical substitutes and shortcuts. Thrifty, she was, in the extreme.

Along with the talk from the missionary, Joan Judd, was a second memorable and life-changing event for me that was instrumental in my journey to fulfilment. A social worker from the 'Christian Social Council' came to tell us about the work of their organisation. She spoke about the placement into Christian homes of children that had been given up for adoption. After her address she asked if there were any questions. There were several and the one that caused my heart to race was the reply to the query about the number of children placed in one family. The answer was, "No limit. Siblings were never separated even if there were two or more born of the same mother and given up for adoption, or if the adoptive parents had had a child of their own after being given a child from CSC."

Following three miscarriages early in our marriage and no subsequent pregnancies, we had applied to Child Welfare as potential adoptive parents. We were told that the maximum number of babies given for adoption to successful applicants was two as there were more qualifying couples than adoptable children. This was one of their strict rules at that time, even if an unmarried mother later had another child to be given up for adoption, it would not be placed with its sibling if the adoptive parents had already been given two children. We had adopted two little boys, Tony and Jonathan from Child Welfare and were told that there would be no more. We would now love to have a little girl or two to complete our family. CSC now offered the fulfilling for the emptiness I felt within my life.

I waited impatiently for the end of the meeting then chased after the speaker as she left. I caught up with her before she got to her car and told her that we already had adopted two little boys through Child Welfare but would love to have a little girl to complete our family, even if the child were imperfect. Child Welfare, at that time kept babies for a minimum of two months before placing them to check that there were no deformities or abnormalities and therefore fit to be placed for adoption. The Representative from CSC had told us that they had no such ruling.

She gave me a contact number to phone to apply to the head of CSC and we went our separate ways, I in great excitement and anticipation. When I got home, I phoned Martin with the news, and then the number given to me and was told that we would receive an application form to be completed and returned to their office. If we were successful applicants, we would be contacted to come into their offices for an interview.

The application forms arrived in the post the following day and a week after returning them we received a phone call asking us to come in for an interview with the liaison officer.

When we got there, she acknowledged receipt of our application form, but informed us that there were several incongruities, which she queried. "Under the question for 'Church affiliation' you've simply filled in 'Christian', which church do you attend?" she asked.

"We don't go to church, but we send Tony every week to the Methodist Sunday School and Jon will go there too when he's ready for Sunday School. I belong to the Young Mother's Fellowship at the Methodist Church. I go there every second Tuesday," I replied.

She frowned, then added, "Furthermore, in this application form you omitted to enter the dates of your children's baptisms. Why is that?" she asked.

"Well, they haven't been christened," I replied.

"Why have the children not been Baptised?" she asked again.

"Is it important?" I asked. "What is a splash of water going to do for them? We send them to a Christian Sunday School and in time they will be confirmed." I did not add, *"Then ideally, we will send them for exposure to Judaism, Islam, Hinduism, or whatever other religions there are, and they can find God for themselves if He is to be found".*

She shook her head, saying, "You obviously don't know what it means to be Christian and as a Christian organisation we are committed to place children for adoption into Christian homes. For a start, go and speak to the minister of the Church you're associated with and have the boys baptised, then we will reconsider your application."

I was confused by all that. We were not Indians, Chinese, Japanese, or Jews, but white South Africans of Dutch descent, and educated in top English schools, so of course we were Christian. If having the boys christened was so important to them, then so be it.

Martin went back to work, and I proceeded to phone around to all the churches in the area. First, the Baptists. They baptise and I suppose that's christening, so that's the route to take.

"Good afternoon. We would like to have our children christened. Can you please tell us what to do?"

"What are their names and ages?"

"Tony is five and Jon is two," I replied. "I know that we should have had them done as babies, but is it too late?"

"We don't christen babies or small children in the Baptist Church," was the secretary's response. "We practice believer's baptism, so after children have gone through Sunday school, they go through the confirmation class, profess their faith in Jesus Christ and then are baptised around the age of sixteen."

So next I phoned the Methodist Church. After all, Tony was in their Sunday School, and I attended the young mother's Fellowship. I spoke to the secretary, and she put me through to the minister. I told him that we had never had Tony or Jon christened as babies and added the white lie that the grandparents were now insisting on them being done. "What is the standard age for christening?" I asked. "Is it too late to have them done now?"

"There's no set age for baptism," he replied. "It is more common to baptise the babies of church members, but I have baptised teenagers and an adult if they request it and have not been baptised as infants. Have you and your husband been baptised?" he asked.

"Yes, Martin was christened in the Dutch Reformed Church, and I was christened as a baby. I think it was also in the Dutch Reformed Church, but I'm not sure. Does it matter?" I asked.

"No, it doesn't matter," he replied. "Christian baptism is recognised by all Christian churches across the different denomination, but in the case of the baptism of infants or young children, at least one of their parents need to be a professing Christian and therefore baptised," he added. "I would be happy to baptise your boys, but for you to gain better understanding of the meaning of baptism I would require you to attend a membership orientation class. I hope to be starting one soon. I will let you know when it will be."

We left it at that. I certainly did not want to attend any teenage confirmation classes. I just wanted the boys christened to satisfy the adoption agency. With remembering that we had both been christened in the DRC, I decided to try them and looked up the number in the telephone book.

The secretary put me through to the Dominee. "You may have been christened in the DRC, but you don't attend this church nor do your children come to our Sunday School. When you both come to church regularly here and enrol your children in our Sunday School, we may consider christening them. It is most unusual though as we usually christen small babies born to members of our church," he said, then added, "I would advise you to approach the church that you do attend." So that was that!

I next tried the Anglican Church, with a similar, but far gentler let-down and advice again to approach the Methodist Church as my best option. Which indeed was the only option, it seemed.

A week later Reverend Pedersen, the Methodist Minister, phoned me to tell me that he was starting the New Members Orientation Class the following week. I told him that I did not fancy going along to any teenage confirmation classes. He assured me that it was not a confirmation class but nine adults wanting to be received into membership of the Pinelands Methodist Church. One person was on transfer from the Anglican Church, two from the Presbyterian Church, a couple who have moved into the area, and four others simply wanting their membership recognised.

"As a matter of fact, three of them you know from Young Mother's Fellowship," he added cheerfully. "If you join us that would make ten all together. Come along next Thursday evening at 8 o'clock. We will be meeting in the hall where you gather for YMF."

Thursday came… and went. All day Thursday I kept remembering my last day of Sunday School and the closer it got to 8 o'clock the more fearful I became. I couldn't do it. I panicked and opted out.

On Friday morning one of the YMF members who lived close by called on me. "We were expecting you at the New Members Orientation Class last night and we missed you. What happened?" she asked.

"I chickened out," was my reply.

"Oh, that's a pity. It was great fun," said Denise. "As it was the introductory session, Erek, the Minister, introduced Nick, who is one of the Church Stewards and the youth leader. He facilitated the fellowship segment, and Erek leads the Bible Study."

"First Nick got us to pair up with someone we didn't know. There were nine of us and as we were an odd number, I joined Pat and Jenny. You and I would have been paired," She added. (Oh dear, I'd let them down not being there.) "We were to get to know our partner by establishing three things about them: their name, what they enjoyed doing and what they were hoping for. Then each in turn was to introduce our partner to the rest of the group." That sounded as bad as it could be. I would have hoped that I could fade quietly into a corner and listen. "Then," Denise continued, "Erek, took over and told us a bit about himself, his hobbies and his hopes. He then introduced us to the nine-week study entitled 'Who is Jesus?' and gave us each the study manual. He gave me a copy to pass on to you and said he is looking forward to seeing you next week." "I'll pick you up at quarter-to-eight, O.K?"

"Right," was my sheepish reply. What could I say? I took the booklet and after she left, I browsed through it. It looked interesting, but I puzzled over the title of the study – 'Who Is Jesus?' Surely it should be 'Who *Was* Jesus?' I cringe at bad grammar.

A week later – there was no way of backing out. I had a glass of wine with my dinner, and another after dinner to give me courage, and yet another to steady my nerves, and another slug for good measure. Now I was floating. I could face the masses – I hoped. Denise called and I picked up my 'Who is Jesus?' Study Manual and a copy of the only Bible in the house, which I got from the visiting Jehovah's Witnesses who had called a few months back.

We arrived at the Church Hall and made our way through the minor-hall and up a narrow winding staircase to what was called 'The Upper Room'. I was gripped by fear as that made an escape difficult. There was the Reverend Pedersen smiling at me. "Hello Joan, I'm glad you made it. This is Nick," he said as the other man came forward.

"I can't stand up and introduce myself," I said, and I felt my lip beginning to tremble and my eyes mist over. I was scared to the core of my being! He must have caught my alcohol rich breath and staggered back then with raised eyebrows he glanced at Nick who had also caught the fumes and was obviously amused.

"That's alright," said Reverend Pedersen. "You don't have to stand, just sit to speak when you have to," he said. "What's that book?" he asked changing the subject and taking the Jehovah's Witness Bible from my trembling hands.

"It's a Bible," I replied.

"Oh, it's a Jehovah's Witness Bible," he remarked. "Here, you can use one of the Church Bibles," he said, and handed me one of the Bibles lying on top of the piano. He then placed my Bible there and said, "You can use ours instead, and leave that one at home next time."

I sat down next to Denise and watched as the other members came upstairs chatting happily. I began to feel sick. What do I do? I can't throw up on the carpet and I can't push my way past those making their way up that narrow staircase to get to the cloakroom downstairs. If I manage to get out in time, I'll never come back again, not even to YMF. "Oh God if you want me to stay. Please take the nausea away." Quite suddenly I felt better and strangely calmer. I actually began to enjoy my first session of 'Who is Jesus?' I didn't make a further fool of myself, not that night or on any of the following eight evenings, nor did I feel the need to anaesthetise myself again with alcohol.

Each session was divided into two segments. The first a fellowship or creative session led by Nick, the second a Bible Study led by Rev Pedersen. I could not bring myself to call him Erek as all the others did. The Bible Study sections took us through various Biblical references to the birth of Jesus; his pre-existence, which was, for me, mind-boggling; his teachings; healing ministry; trial; death; resurrection; and promise of his return. All astonishing and strangely inspiring.

The fellowship segments I thoroughly enjoyed. Each was related to different phases in the life of Jesus. One time we each made a nativity scene from plasticine. Another time we formed four groups to imagine and re-enact the reaction of the guards, the anger of the pharisees, the astonishment of the disciples on finding the tomb empty and the delight of the followers at the after-death appearances of Jesus. At the final meeting we ended with a parfait and pudding party. It was after the study of Jesus second coming and the marriage feast.

That Pudding Party celebrated the end of the New Members Orientation Study. That had another major impact on my journey to transformation. That morning I had a hospital appointment to have chest x-rays taken as I had been suffering for several weeks with a persistent cough, which no medication alleviated. At the hospital my chest was x-rayed, but the radiologists kept examining and discussed the x-rays plates among themselves then called me back to repeat or retake more x-rays from different angles. Finally, they checked with two consultants. Eventually they gave me the thick envelope with all the x-ray pictures and told me to go immediately to my doctor, saying that they had phoned him, and he was expecting me.

Back in the car I looked at the x-rays and all I saw were white ribs, my spinal column and two large roughly triangular patches which, of course were my lungs. They were completely black. 'Oh dear' I thought. 'Those are my lungs and solid with disease.'

Back at the surgery the secretary informed me that the doctor was on his was and to wait my turn. Within minutes the doctor came in and beckoned me to come through. "I wasn't the first," I said, "The others were all here before me."

"Never mind, come," He insisted ushering me through. He took the envelope from me and held the x-ray pictures one by one up to the light, inspecting each carefully. I watched in silence, then eventually he turned to me looking stern.

"How long have I got?" I asked.

"What do you mean?" was his reply.

"How long have I got to live? How far has the cancer spread? Can you tell?"

"Cancer? Is that what you think It Is?" he chuckled.

"Well, what is it then?" I asked. "Why were the radiologists and consultants so concerned? Why did they keep calling me back to take more x-rays? Why do these pictures show two solid, black lungs?"

"Black doesn't mean clogged solid, but crystal clear," he chuckled. "What worried them was a tiny white spot on the one picture which doesn't show up again on any of the other x-rays. It could be scar tissue or it may be a blemish on the negative," he explained. "I'm glad you were given a fright," he added. "Perhaps now you will stop smoking! I've warned you often enough."

"Why did you send me for x-rays?" I asked. "What did you think that it could be?"

"I thought that it may be tuberculosis, which would mean you would go off to a TB clinic, but fortunately, it's not that. Just *stop smoking* and your cough will hopefully clear up."

"But what if that mark on the x-ray is the beginning of cancer?" I asked.

"Well, we wait and see. If it is, it will grow and spread." That's the kind of doctor he was, scare his patients into a healthier lifestyle, and it worked, for I never smoked another cigarette from that day on.

It had certainly given me a shock and what's more, it got me thinking of the hereafter. If I died -- *when* I die, for I surely would one day – would I go to heaven or would I go to hell... it there were such places, and certainly the orientation classes had me pondering on eternity.

That evening I went to the final meeting of the New Members Orientation Course with mixed emotions – relief that I was not terminally ill; uncertainties concerning the afterlife; excitement in anticipation of preparing for the party; and sad that the course had now come to an end. I was really enjoying it.

We had each brough along ingredients to create parfaits or puddings for the party. After the Bible Study which was on the Wedding Banquet of Jesus as the Bridegroom and the Church as his Bride, we made our way down to the kitchen to prepare the Pudding Party. All the ingredients were spread out on the table – A trifle; a 2-litre tub of ice-cream; a bowl of mixed tropical fruits; a jug of chocolate sauce, and another of strawberry syrup; a tub of whipped cream; a bowl of nuts; sliced cake; jelly; shortbread... The urn was bubbling, and the men were setting out the chairs while one of the ladies was setting out cups and pudding bowls. Another was uncovering the dishes.

I went to fetch the parfait glasses from the cupboard in the corner as I knew which cupboard they were in. In my enthusiasm I yanked open the sliding door of the cupboard where they were stored. Picked up two and turned to put them on the counter. There was an almighty *BANG!*

I though a bomb had exploded, and we were all dead. I opened my eyes and before me stood Rev Pedersen, smiling. 'Whew! What a relief,' flashed through my mind. 'If he's here too I've gone to heaven not to hell.'

"Sorry, I should have warned you. That cupboard door is loose and falls out with a crash if you don't hold onto it," he said. "Don't worry. It's easily put back. David has promised to come across and repair it."

Life and death. Heaven or hell? Emptiness or fulfilment. Anticipating a funeral or preparations for a party? That day had indeed presented much food for thought.

* * *

'My thoughts are not your thoughts,
neither are your ways my ways,' declares the Lord.
'For as the heavens are higher than the earth,
so are my ways higher than your ways.
and my thoughts than your thoughts.'

(Isaiah 55:8,9)

Chapter 6
Holey, Wholly, Holy & Whole

Three days later, on Sunday evening, 1st December 1974, I was preparing to be received into membership of Pinelands Methodist Church. I saw this as a momentous event yet a brazen act on my part, for I was not a churchgoer, so how could I be so bold as to be received into church membership. I saw no way of changing my demeanour without hypocrisy. I would be living a lie and I could not see that as being compatible with church membership. Was not church membership indicating a relationship with God?

To my recollection, I had only gone to church on five occasions. Those were not to worship an unknown God but to attend the weddings of my sisters, my cousins, and on the last three occasions, first to hear our banns being called prior to our wedding, then for my own wedding and lastly, that time a year ago, when Connie had sent me in to the service prior to our end-of-year party for Young Mother's Fellowship. That was the time when the visitor had come in and sat down beside me: The one whom everyone else ignored and later denied having seen, making me out to be a liar or hallucinating

I had not taken part in the Communion Service that morning, but this evening I had fulfilled all the requirements for church membership so I would go to 'The Table of the Lord' to receive Communion in the Bread and Grape Juice for the first time.

In anticipation of this momentous occasion. I had scrubbed up well, taking a leisurely bubble bath, washed my hair in a fragrant shampoo, put on my favourite, 'special occasions' smart blue dress and I was ready. But was I? I stood at the window watching the boys playing in the garden outside. Where was Martin? He was not home yet. Would he be back home in time to look after the boys so I could go to church? He had said he would be home in time, but I was not sure that I could trust him to keep that commitment. I looked down at the list of responses we were to make, enabling us to be received into membership.

The first one: *'I have heard the call of Christ and I am answering it.'* I had heard no call. How could I say that I had? That would be a lie – and *in Church* too!? I couldn't do that.

The second response: *'I promise to be faithful in attending worship, Bible Study and Fellowship within the Methodist Church.'* Well, fellowship yes, that would be fulfilled at Young Mother's Fellowship meetings, but I don't want to make a fool of myself in a Bible Study

Group, and can I promise to start coming to church every Sunday?

I could not be sure of keeping those required promises, and more importantly, I could not claim to having heard the call of Christ. I was not even sure that he was real. With that my whole life unfolded before my eyes, and I saw only failure from infancy throughout my life. I had not been an adorable child. Didn't my mother continuously chastise me? I had not been a diligent student. Hadn't I been lazy, not studied and only scraped through each test and exam without having swotted for them? I was obviously not a beloved wife, for why did Martin go to work parties without me? I wasn't even sure if Martin would bother to be home in time tonight? I was not a good mother – in fact, I was not a mother at all. Three miscarriages and two adopted children - not mine. Now wanting to bring a third into this dysfunctional family... and what about the here and now? I could not go to church and make promises without lying.

Rather than lie in church I will simply not go to the reception service tonight. I will possibly not have the nerve to go back to YMF either. I will simply have to plod on in the downward spiral to my natural end. A feeling of despair and hopelessness swept over me. I wanted to die, to end my life, for I was a dismal failure. I was ready to end it, but what then? If I topped myself I would for sure go straight to hell if there were such a place, and I could not take that gamble. Well, there was only one thing to do. If Jesus is real, he will hear me. If not or he doesn't care, he will ignore me, and I simply plod on to the end.

My whole being cried out in a silent cry, 'Jesus, if you are real and hear me, please take my life! I don't care how you do it, I just don't want to go on and I don't want to go to hell – I want to be *with you!*'

It was as though a curtain was lifted. The sky, the garden, the world was suddenly lighter, brighter, radiant – and Jesus stood before me, "I'll be *with you,*" he said. He stood less than an arms-length away and a little to my left. He was – no, *is* beautiful, for I saw that he is beyond time and space. Love streamed from his eyes, from his whole being, a love that I had never known, could not fully grasp, but it did indeed flood my body, my soul, my entire being.

"You can't possibly love me. No one, not my husband, not even my mother has ever loved me *that* much. You obviously don't know me," was my response.

"I've known you from the beginning," he smiled.

"The beginning of what?" I wondered. "From my birth? From the start of my life? From the beginning of civilisation, of human existence, of the world, of creation?" but he gave no answer. I was amazed that he spoke to me in my tongue – not in High Dutch. Not in Hebrew, Aramaic, Greek, posh or archaic King James Bible English.

He is more beautiful than any human being I have ever seen, not as depicted in so many paintings or representations of the man Jesus: an emaciated figure drooping on a cross or dressed in the coarse robes of a typical biblical character of that time, but a timeless, strong, and muscular, masculine, yet tender figure, clothed in a robe of fine cloth.

"I'll be with you to the end," he had said, and with that I felt a tingling warmth, like golden oil, flowing over and through me, from the top of my head, touching, enveloping, and transforming every cell of my body, down to the tips of my toes. I felt that I was being reshaped, remade.

"So, *this* is the Holy Spirit!" my newly awakened soul proclaimed. I had listened to Erek pronounce the benediction at the close of each meeting of the 'Who is Jesus?' study. I knew: 'The Father' – that's God; 'The Son' – that's Jesus, but who on earth was this 'Holy Ghost', or 'Holy Spirit'? Now I knew, and he filled me from top to bottom. In fact, I knew him in the Biblical sense, for I was fully filled, fulfilled and tingling with sensual gratification! I knew that this was the way in which Jesus would be with me – 'to the end'.

"The end of what?" I wondered. The end of the day? The end of my life, the end of the world? The end of time?" again he did not answer, but it did not matter. I knew at once that there now would be no end to life or to this glorious new relationship with Jesus. It was as though I had died to my former life and been reborn into the heavenly family as a child of God.

I heard a sound of voices singing. It was beautiful and almost like the tinkling of bells. Jesus turned, and in turning drew me with him looking to the source of the singing. Above the trees at the edge of the garden the sky was filled with angels. They were singing praises to Jesus for having redeemed another lost soul from the clutches of the enemy. They were not singing in any earthly language, but I understood it anyway. I realised that it was the language of the angels.

I became aware of an angry scuffling behind me in the region of the fireplace. It was diabolical, but Jesus ignored it and so did I for I knew that I belonged to Jesus, encapsulated in the protective sphere of his love. The devil had no hold on me – anymore.

I don't know how long it was, for I had been enfolded in eternity. One minute is as one hour, one day, one never ending lifetime. Jesus faded from my sight, but I still felt his presence with me, as he is with me now and always will be though I see him not. He said it and whether I feel it or not, it is so.

I was enjoying the newness of life in and all around me. The lawn was alive. The trees were alive. The foliage and shrubs and flowers were alive. There was a spark of life in all the garden, it was as though there were little living beings scurrying up and down the trees and through the grass as life form, carrying nutrients, chemicals, air up and down to every cell, leaf, petal. Everything was breathing life. The sky had taken on a new vitality, the clouds were carrying out their mission. Everything had a purpose and was faithfully carrying out its function.

The phone rang and I went to answer It. It was Connie calling to tell me that we would be receiving Holy Communion at the service this evening, and that each of those being received into membership could be accompanied by a partner or friend. As she knew that I would be on my own, she said that she would accompany me to 'The Lord's Table.'

"That's alright, Connie," I replied. "I'm not alone but thank you anyway."

"Oh, is Martin coming with you?" she asked.

"No," I replied. "He'll be here with the children. I'll explain it to you sometime."

Martin was not home yet, but it no longer bothered me. I knew that all would be well. Nothing mattered. As I stood enjoying newness of life the car came up the driveway and Martin was home. He was still locked into the world as it had been for me. He came in still infolded in a miasma of worldliness. I couldn't tell him what had happened for he would not understand.

I went to church as though I was floating on a cloud. We were to gather in the hall for final instructions and prayer.

Erek greeted us all and looked at me strangely as though I was an interloper, then began handing out our certificates of membership one by one. He stopped in the middle of that, looked around, looked at me again with a puzzled expression, then said, "I'll tell you what. I'll leave your certificates here on the top of the piano, you can collect them later rather than being hampered holding them in your hands."

'He's probably stopped at mine,' I thought. 'I'm sure that he doesn't recognise me.' I went across to the piano and was delighted to see that my guess was confirmed as my certificate was the one on the top of the pile. That verified for me that I was no longer who or what I had been my whole life before Jesus, or Holy Spirit transformed me.

We all went as a group together and across the lawn and into the church to be received into membership and sat, as we were instructed, in the two front pews. I was delighted to be sitting in the same spot that I had sat in a year before at the Young Mother's Fellowship close of year service. The atmosphere was quite different and though it was now evening the church, like my living room and the world too was lighter and brighter. Indeed, there was an atmosphere of heaven in the church as a mass of angels filled the space above the Communion Table. They were similar, but not the same company of angels that had been above our garden singing praises to Jesus earlier that evening.

When the time came to make our responses to the questions asked by Erek before being received into membership, he asked, "Have you heard the call of Christ?"

I was now able, with great enthusiasm, to respond, "I have heard the call of Christ and I am answering it!" My body tingled with delight.

To the next statement I was now able to say with confidence, "I promise to attend worship regularly, to join in fellowship within the church, to partake in Bible Study and to witness to life in Christ."

I went up to the Communion rail with the rest of the group. They were all joined by their 'significant other', but Connie did not come up with me as she had said she would. But it did not matter to me as I did not expect or need anyone else. I was filled with God's Spirit and awed by the holy aura filling the church.

Back in the hall for tea Erek gave us each, together with our certificates of membership of the Methodist Church, an inscribed card with the words:

> *In Response to God's Love for Me...*
> *I Receive the Lord Jesus Christ as my Saviour and Lord.*
> *I accept the forgiveness He offers*
> *and the new life He imparts.*
> *I give to Him all that I am and all that I have.*
> *And I offer myself to be of service in His Kingdom,*
> *And in the manner of His choosing.*
> *Signed.................................... Dated...................*

Connie came over, and looking at me strangely she asked, "Joan?'

"Yes?" I beamed back at her.

"I'm sorry, I had promised to go up with you to Communion, but I didn't recognise you," she said. "I wondered who this person was, being received into membership. Erek has just told me that he too didn't recognise you and thought that you, being timid and nervous, had sent your sister to take your place. What's happened to you? You're *glowing!*"

I secretly rejoiced in that further confirmation that I was indeed transformed. I wasn't *me* anymore - or maybe I was now *really* me. Fulfilled and wholly whole.

"I can't tell you about it now, but I will some time." I replied. How could I tell anyone what had happened? They wouldn't believe me. They would say, 'Who does she think *she* is that Jesus should come to *her*?' Well, it's not who *I* am but who Jesus is!

* * *

Be strong and of good courage,
be not afraid, neither be thou dismayed:
for the Lord thy God is with thee
whithersoever thou goest.

(Joshua 1:9 AV)

Chapter 7
New Life for Old

That night, as I recalled the events of the day, I lay awake not wanting to fall asleep. I was anxious that if I slept, I would wake in the morning having lost the sparkle of new life. But I did fall asleep and awoke in the morning singing praise to Jesus and tingling all over, just as I had the night before. I was not sure if the song of praise was a continuation of my dream, but I was bubbling over with joy as I realised that my ecstasy remained. I had been adopted; no, *reborn* into God's family. How could I dare to tell anyone that?

Reflecting on my life as it had been, I suddenly realised with a shock the wickedness of what I had been and done over the years and throughout my life. Jesus had told me that he had known me from the beginning, but did The Father know and would He have accepted me?

"Please, Jesus, don't tell God what I've been and done, lest he take the Holy Spirit from me."

'He knows,' came the inner voice. Of course, and because of Jesus, He loved me too – unconditionally.

I remembered with shame, how I had once stood at the kitchen window and sworn at God to see if he would react. That would prove to me that there was a God who heard or cared what I said. Well, nothing happened. At the time it proved to me that either there was no God, or he did not care.

We had been strictly brought up to respect our elders. My mother had never permitted us to use God's name except in prayer, for she believed that to do so was blasphemous and would incur God's wrath. Even to use the expression 'good heavens' carried the terror of being struck by lightning. I had often been punished when my mother construed my high-spirited retorts as disrespect. Now I remembered that I had deliberately sworn at God. "Oh Lord, why didn't you strike me dead?" I asked.

"My dear child, how could I kill that which was not yet alive? I loved you then as I do now and longed for you to turn to me so I would give you fullness of life." a gentle voice whispered in my head, and with those words caressing my soul, a new flood of love enfolded me in a warm embrace.

I bounced out of bed, dressed, and prepared breakfast for the family. It was strange that not only Erek and Connie, but several others at church last evening had asked me what had happened to me, but Martin and the children were still the same as they had always been and did not notice any change in me. I said nothing but served them breakfast and saw them off to work and school. After dropping Jon off at nursery school, I drove to the shopping centre and stood outside the local branch of the Central News Agency, waiting for the doors to open so that I could buy a copy of the Living Bible.

That was the translation that Elise had told me that she read from when it was her turn to read during the 'Who is Jesus?' course. It impressed me as it lacked the archaic language of my old school Bible that I had left behind when I left home, or that Jehovah Witness Bible that I had been given by them. But the Living Bible was written in the language that I was familiar with, and the way Jesus too had spoken to me. Erek had not taken that Bible from her and given her a copy of the Church Bible as he had when I had arrived with my Jehovah Witness Bible.

The doors of the CNA were eventually opened, and I headed straight for the Bibles displayed on the shelf at the back of the shop. I picked up a hard covered copy of the Living Bible, and it felt so comfortable in my hands. I paid for it and hurried out. There was a homeless man sitting in the corner between the café and block of flats across from the CNA. He looked dejected and grubby, with a chunk of bread in one hand and small carton of milk beside him. I wanted to go over and tell him that God loved him. But thought that I had better not. What would he say? What would people passing by think?

I hurried home to feast my hungry soul from my newly purchased treasure. I opened at random, and the top of the page was headed 'John'. My old self would have turned to page one of the beginning of books that I was going to read, so in the past it would have been Genesis chapter 1, verse 1 … now the 'new me' opened at random ¾ way through my new Bible. It opened at a page headed simply 'John'.

I began to read, and what did I discover? It related to the creation of the world, and almost a repeat of what I had read every New Year's Day through my teen years.

It had then been my New Year's resolution to get into the discipline of reading my Bible. Of course, like most New Year's resolutions, it hadn't lasted even a week. On January 1st, 2nd, 3rd and 4th I had read Genesis Chapter 1 to 4. I had been puzzled by the similarity yet difference between chapters 1 and 2, then in chapter 3 I began to get bored with the archaic language and by the time I reached Genesis Chapter 5 I gave up as I could not be bothered with the endless list of who begat whom. So, being acquainted with Genesis Chapter 1: *'In the beginning God created...'* followed by the repetition of *'And God said...'* as God created each part of the world, I was astonished to find that the start of what was headed 'John', said that Jesus along with God, created the world. I read: *'1 Before anything else existed there was Christ, with God. 2 He has always been alive and is himself God. 3 He created everything there is— nothing exists that he didn't make.'*

WOW – Jesus was *there* with God creating the world! Just as it said in Genesis 1: *'1 In the beginning God created the heaven and the earth. 2 And the earth was without form, and void; and darkness was upon the face of the deep. And the Spirit of God moved upon the face of the waters.*

I read on and there again, I compared both this section headed 'John' 1:4 *Eternal life is in him, and this life gives light to all mankind. 5His life is the light that shines through the darkness—and the darkness can never extinguish it,'* with Genesis 1:3 *And God said, Let there be light: and there was light. 4And God saw the light, that it was good: and God divided the light from the darkness.*

Was there no end to the serendipitous surprises along this journey of New Life? So, I read on to the end of 'John'. I found the Bible exciting beyond belief. As

Jesus had spoken to me so now this new Bible of mine was also speaking to me in plain English. I read to the end of 'John', and I could no longer hold my excitement. I phoned the Church Office and asked to speak to Erek. "There's a section towards the back of the Bible called, 'John'. Have you ever read it?" I asked. "It's absolutely amazing. You've got to read it if you haven't already done so!"

I could hear that he was chuckling as he replied, "Yes, I've read it and it is wonderful."

This was so exciting, I turned back to the beginning and found that Genesis now also spoke to me in my familiar tongue. There was a new freshness and vibrancy about it. I read on through chapter 5, which had always tripped me up before, but now I found it extremely interesting. Then on through Noah and the flood and on through to Abram and Lot. I was delighted with all the exciting stories of real people with their hopes and fears, struggles and joys, challenges and devotion to God.

I realised that I too had been like some of them, rebellious and totally unlovable. I felt that I would burst with all the love that God was pouring into me. I felt like saying, "Stop! I can't hold any more or I'll burst."

Not forgetting my responsibilities, I quickly made the beds, tidied the house and it was time to fetch Jon from Nursery School, then home to prepare lunch before Tony got home. Shortly after lunch there was a knock at the door and there to my surprise was Erek. Of course, he wanted to know what had happened to me, and I told him. He was not shocked by my daring to presume that I had received a visit from Jesus, nor was he stunned by my telling him that I had been reborn as a child of God. He assured me that it was not only believable, but scriptural. "We are born physically into the world, but the Bible tells us that we need to be born spiritually, thereby becoming children of God," he said.

I knew that and had read it myself only this morning in Jesus' chat with Nicodemus. I was delighted to have that affirmation from Erek, for I thought that no one would accept that I dared to believe that I had become God's child, as only Jesus is the Son of God, so how dare we call ourselves God's children? Well, we are!

He went on to say that he would be in touch with the CSC in Port Elizabeth to tell them the news and to assure them that the boys would be baptised to fulfil their requirements, so we could be put on the waiting list to adopt a baby girl.

"No. I don't want another child now," I said. "It wasn't a little girl that is missing from my life. It was the absence of God that created a vacuum in me. I am now fulfilled by Jesus' love, His indwelling Holy Spirit and extatically happy as I am."

When Erek stood up to leave, he said, "Let's pray together." At the door he took my hands in his and gave thanks to God for what he had done through the 'Who is Jesus?' course and asked that the baby girl we wanted would be given soon to complete our family.

I was bursting with love for everyone and wanted to fling my arms around Erek and give him a fat kiss, but of course, I couldn't do that anymore than I could hug the homeless man outside the CNA this morning. I was however a little annoyed that he had not grasped what I was saying about not wanting another child.

After he left, I apologised to God for being annoyed at Erek's misunderstanding. Hadn't it been for the want of a baby girl that this miracle had happened? If it was God's plan for our lives, I told God that we would happily accept a baby girl, "but please, Jesus, I need to be sure that she is *your* choice of a baby for me, not ours through unfulfilled desire. I'll know she is your choice if she has your loving eyes, Jesus, and your dark hair, and I'll call her Karin, 'beloved one'."

That night on going to be bed, Martin became affectionate. I knew the signs. "Oh, Lord! What now? How do I tell him that I can no longer allow this?"

"Why not?" came the reply as a now familiar voice in my head. "Was it not I who gave the gift of sexuality, not only for procreation in plants and animals but for fulfilment, affection and joy in human beings?"

"Well, OK then. You said it." And that night and ever since I enjoyed the act more than I ever had before. I then realised that sexuality and spirituality were closely aligned. Well, weren't they? Union, completion, conception, production, reproduction, creation, procreation, recreation, re-creation, fulfilment!

* * *

You have searched me, Lord, and you know me.
You know when I sit and when I rise;
you perceive my thoughts from afar.
You discern my going out and my lying down;
you are familiar with all my ways....
When I awake, I am still with you.

(Psalm 139:1-3, 18b – NIV)

Chapter 8
Growing Pains

The following day at Young Mother's Fellowship, I sailed in with new confidence, a spring in my step and joy in my soul. I was now truly one of them. Those who had been in Church on Sunday evening, and that was most of them, knew that something wonderful had happened to me. Those who had not been there saw by my demeanour that I was different. They all gathered around and wanted to know what had happened. I told them and was not surprised that they all accepted the news with delight as had Erek.

"What did Martin say about it?" asked Connie. She was surprised when I said that I had not told him what had happened and astounded that he had not remarked on the change in me.

"I didn't tell him because he wouldn't understand," I explained. I did not add that he did not notice any change in me for he is so wrapped up in himself.

"You must tell him!" she insisted. "It is in sharing with others that your conversion and commitment are securely established," she said.

That evening when Martin got home, I told him to sit down for a minute as I had something important to tell him. He reluctantly complied as I recounted the events of Sunday evening before I went to church to be received into membership. He listened with scepticism, and impatience. When I had finished, his only comment was, "That's not possible. You're *my wife*." Got up and walked out of the room.

What was that supposed to mean? Did he think that Jesus had to have his permission before delivering me from the clutches of Satan, or that I should have asked Martin before offering myself to Jesus? Or should Jesus have consulted him before pouring His Spirit into me?

Despite Martin's lack of enthusiasm, I was eager to share with my family the exciting news of what had happened to me. I wrote to my parents, to Betty, Clara, and Junior of how I had completed the 'Who is Jesus?' Course, and not able to make the required responses of hearing the call of Christ, I had confessed (omitting the death wish) that I wanted to be with Jesus *when* I die, whereupon Jesus stood before me, telling me that he would be with *me* from then on, and that he had poured his Holy Spirit into me. I added in the letter to my parents, that I was looking forward to their annual visit in February. To Clara and Junior, I said that I was looking forward to seeing them over the Easter school holidays when we would be up in the Transvaal to see them and the in-laws. Betty I would see when we went to fetch the baby that we were to be offered through the Christian Social Council at their adoption home in Port Elizabeth, for P.E. was where Betty now lived.

A week later I was amazed at the replies I got from each of those family members. They were not like the enthusiasm I received from my new spiritual 'parents', Erek & Connie, or my brothers and sisters in Christ in the Church family. Mum's response was: "My dear, I'm so proud of you. Daddy says that you are mistaken that we were planning to come to visit you next month. In fact, he insists that it's our turn to go up to Clara and to see Junior and their families. I *thought* that we were coming to you, but I think that Daddy feels intimidated by your news." Oh dear, I thought that Daddy, whom I had always felt favoured me most of his children, would be delighted.

The reply from Betty was: "I haven't the faintest idea what you mean by what you call your wonderful news. *I* have some exciting news though. I've redecorated my kitchen and painted the walls cherry red, made matching curtains in custard yellow, cream and cherry stripes. It looks yummy. You'll see it when you come down here. It's good news about the baby you're expecting to adopt." I smiled at her typical excitement over news of her home decorating, and lack of understanding of spirituality. It surprised me, as she was the one in our family who had spiritual experiences and a sensitivity to the ghost. To the end of her life at age seventy-eight, she never understood my spiritual devotion as I tried to share it with her.

The letter from Clara surprised me the most. She wrote: "That is wonderful news! I'm so happy for you. The same thing happened to me a year back, but I haven't told anybody about it. Your letter gives me the courage to do so. I was having marital problems, and a friend of mine suggested that I go and speak to her minister as he had helped her some time back. I made an appointment with him and his advice to me was: 'You need Jesus in your life.' (Go to a minister and he'll say that. Go to a doctor and he'll prescribe anti-depressants...) Anyway, I got home and as I was hanging my washing on the line I said, 'Well Jesus, Rev Green says that I need you in my life, so what do I do?' With that there was Jesus standing before me enfolding me in his love, he said, 'I'll be with you.' I felt loved beyond measure. I was able to cope with the crisis in our marriage, but I haven't told anyone about it. I didn't feel though, as you have, that I received the Holy Spirit."

She later wrote and told me that having been motivated by my letter, she had gone to tell Rev Green of her experience. He had prayed with her to receive the Baptism in the Holy Spirit. She had been overwhelmed by that, spoken in tongues and eager to go out and tell everyone the good news. She also said that the surprise visit from my parents was eventful as they were astonished by her news. Dad had asked her, on the quiet, to tell him more.

Junior's letter stunned me. It was short and hurtful. "If you think that you are special, holier and better than the rest of us, don't bother to write again or come to visit when you're here, and you won't be hearing from me anymore, either." That from the brother who had been my best friend and confidante through our childhood. He kept his threat and never again responded to Christmas cards or birthday wishes that I sent to them, though his wife, who had never corresponded in the past, replied to letters and cards. There was no mention of greetings from him, though.

Years later, we moved back to Johannesburg and went to pay a surprise visit on them. He told me that he had been deeply hurt by the rejection of a marriage proposal to a girl. The reason given being that his family were obviously unbelievers and she, a committed

Christian, felt that she could not marry him, as the Bible warns against being 'unequally yoked' with unbelievers.

My mother-in-law's comment on my news was simply, "Congratulations. We're pleased to hear that the boys are being christened next month."

That was not the end of the criticism and rejection of my news. Even members of the church were judgemental. I was pleased by Connie's invitation to join her Bible Study group. They were all older women, mostly from the Women's Auxiliary. I found them to be a little cliquish. There could be many reasons for that, but they were certainly not hostile.

We met weekly on a Thursday morning going through Mark's Gospel. When we got to the account of Jesus meeting with a group of friends in the home of Mary and Martha, Connie commented that she did not understand why Jesus had commended Mary for choosing the better way after Martha complained about her sitting at Jesus feet and leaving her to prepare and attend to refreshments. Connie commented that of course Martha was the hostess and was expected to serve the guests, but Mary should have helped her.

I remarked, "Of course, Mary chose the better way sitting at Jesus' feet to feed her hungry soul as he taught. Jesus would have been satisfied with a glass of water by his side, and the other guests should have been happy with tea and a biscuit after the meeting."

Connie remarked to the group, avoiding eye contact with me, "I'm getting tired of these 'heavenly mined people who are of no earthly use'." The rest of the women muttered agreement, some glancing across at me. That became a favourite comment of hers as a wave of revival swept our church with Erek leading a second and third 'Who is Jesus?' courses following the first.

Erek dropped by to visit two or three times a week... to find out how I was getting along, to discuss the christening of the boys, to tell me that he had written to CSC to tell them that the children would be baptised and to inform them of my spiritual awakening.

He informed me that he did not like the term 'christening' as it implied that the child was being made a Christian. Baptism, he said was the correct and scriptural term. I was learning a whole new language and referred frequently to my Shorter Oxford English Dictionary and several other tools to clarify a new and unfamiliar spiritual language. I discovered that blessed meant 'blood covered' which was interesting, and that justified was 'just-as-if-I'd not done it'; sanctified meant 'made into a saint'; redeemed meant 'purchasing back what was really mine but had been seized by another' – in other words, we belong to God, but Satan behaves as though we are his. Jesus has bought us back with his lifeblood and now we are blessed, redeemed, justified, sanctified. We get baptized, or in effect drowned (as citizens of the world) and raised to new spiritual life (as citizens of heaven).

With opposition from some of my family, I discovered that the enemy was fighting to win me back. The disturbance that I had been aware of in the hearth on the night of my conversion was a battle that was being waged through my nearest and dearest.

The worst occurrence began a few days after my conversion. I can't remember the cause, but I came under a severe spiritual attack that was physically manifest. It dragged me to the floor, and I lay wrestling with demonic forces that would drag me to the pit of hell. I wanted to tear my newly acquired Bible to shreds, but I resisted and overcame.

It was wonderful how I won through, and I was moved to read the book of Ephesians. I was gladdened to find that it was not through having been rebellious, but I imagine that God had allowed it to happen so that I could learn to triumph over adversity. I began to see the opposition for what it was, and in hindsight I thank

God for those challenges which served to strengthen and equip me for the fight.

* * *

Be strong in the Lord and in his mighty power.
Put on the full armour of God,
so that you can take your stand
against the devil's schemes.

For our struggle is not against flesh and blood,
but against the rulers, against the authorities,
against the powers of this dark world
and against the spiritual forces of evil
in the heavenly realms.

Therefore, put on the full armour of God,
so that when the day of evil comes
you may be able to stand your ground,
and after you have done everything,
to stand.

(Ephesians 6:10b-13 NIV)

Chapter 9
New Life Unfolds

We received a letter from Christian Social Council to inform us that Rev Pedersen had notified them that I had fulfilled their requirements of baptism of the boys. They were pleased to learn that I had been received into Church membership. They went on to say that they would accept our application for adoption if Martin would likewise be received into membership in the Methodist Church.

Erek invited him to the next 'Who is Jesus?' Course, but Martin declined, insisting that he did not need to as he had been confirmed in the Dutch Reformed Church, but CSC were adamant that he comply with their request. As the membership course was by now well under way, Erek said that he would have to wait for the next series to begin.

Several of the husbands of the women who had been on my membership course attended the second one and were converted and fired up as I was. The church was by now abuzz with revival, Erek was ecstatic, and Connie was singing her mantra about heavenly minded fanatics at every opportunity.

Three years passed as Martin continued to resist CSC's directive with various excuses but eventually complied reluctantly, and we were placed on CSC's waiting list. One afternoon shortly thereafter I received a phone call from CSC informing me that they had a baby girl for us. The following morning, we bundled the boys into the car and drove off to Port Elizabeth to fetch the baby. "What are we going to call her?" I asked, knowing already what name I had in mind, but would lead up to it. I started running through the alphabet... "Anne, Alice, Abigail... Barbara, Brenda... Carol, Cindy, Caren... how about Karin?" I offered hopefully, for that was the name that had come to me after I said that I would be willing to receiving another child, but only if it was God's will and in his plan.

"No, it sounds Jewish," said Martin. Eventually the family settled on Cindy. Because Cindy is a pet name, we added Elizabeth to give it class, but Cindy for short as Jonathan said it was easier to say.

Sitting excitedly in the waiting room of CSC a carrycot was brough in and we peered in. There lay a beautiful rosy-cheeked baby with thick, dark brown hair and hazel eyes beaming up at us. "The birth mother has given her the name of Karin, but you can register her by any name of your choice," we were told. Well, that confirmed it for me. She was God's gift to us. I thought

85

of so many of the Biblical characters who had the name given to them by their parents, and the name that God, or Jesus gave them: Abram → Abraham; Sarai → Sarah; Jacob → Israel; Solomon → Jedidiah; Gideon → Mighty-man-of-valour; Mary → O-favoured-one; Jesus → Emmanuel (God-with-us); Simon → Peter; Saul → Paul.

She was indeed a special child. She was two weeks old when we brought her home. Everyone at the church remarked on her outgoing personality and unique spiritual awareness at such a tender age. To name but two incidents which astounded those who were present at the time: the first was when members of Young Mother's fellowship were to gather with their families down at the seaside for a picnic on the beach. We drove down to Bantry Bay. As we emerged from the carpark and seeing the sea for the first time she squealed with delight, throwing her arms out to encompass the vista, she breathed one sound, which was distinctly 'Jahweh', or JHWH, which is the Hebrew name of God.

The group gathered on the beach turned in stunned silence to see this three-month-old baby with a look of sheer rapture on her face as her eyes swept over the panorama. In a whisper Barbara remarked, "She is indeed a special child of God," and those gathered there nodded in agreement.

The second occasion which was witnessed by others was when we gathered at Carol's home for Bible Study. The hostess would look after the children in the playroom while we went into the lounge for Bible Study. We would begin by singing choruses before the Bible Study, then finish with tea. We left the children in the kitchen gathered around Carol as she gave them fruit-juice and biscuits. We were in the living room, singing: 'How great thou art' when the door suddenly swung open. We all turned and there sat Cindy (Karin) then 10-months old. She smiled at us, then crawled into the room and sat in the centre of the circle, and looking at each of us in turn, she beamed as we sang. The hymn came to an end and there was a moment's silence. Then Karin flung her arms wide and sighed, "Halleluiah!"

"Did you hear that!" said one. "Did she say 'Halleluiah'?" asked another. "It certainly sounded like it," said Isabel. "It was indeed," said Barbara. "I always said that there's something special about her."

"What's going on here?" asked Carol coming into the room. "Oh, there are. What are you doing here?" she said, picking Karin up. "Sorry, I didn't notice her slipping away."

There followed a baby boom among the young couples in our church, as each decided to try for another child. After persuasion, and prayer, Keith and Gill had another little boy to the delight of his brothers Peter and Paul. Ken & Jenny had a little girl to add to their family, Hans and Patty had a baby girl and Brian and Sue were blessed with a brother for Meg & Anne.

As the months and years rolled on, I longed to draw closer to God, to learn more of His ways and His will. Perhaps I was simply becoming more sensitive to God's Spirit guiding me and felt blessed in my obedient responses. I sensed an unfolding of God's purpose in my journey of life.

Starting with being overwhelmed by his love. Then in the desire to know more I read whole books of the Bible. That was exciting, but not enough, so I joined Connie's Bible Study group. I found that group rather judgemental, so I joined the young women's Bible Study group. That did not fully satisfy my hunger for God's Word, so I enrolled at Bible College.

We were to read through the whole Bible in year, a book a week. Reading through Isaiah I was startled by a verse in Isaiah which was strangely highlighted, hinting God's plan for me but revealed only years later.

The following year I enrolled with the University of South Africa, registering in the Theology Department to take my first two modules: Biblical Studies and Systematic Theology. I was delighted that for the first time I not only enjoyed studying but got encouraging feedback and excellent marks.

As if that was not enough, I was told about a Tape Library at the Anglican Church, so I began borrowing tapes from there. I picked up one tape a week from the Tape library and feasted hungrily on the diet of spiritual wisdom, digesting, first a series by a well-known Bible Scholar, expounding each phrase of the Lord's Prayer. Another series expanded upon the parables of Jesus. I glutted on the teachings of my favourite lecturer.

Sarah, who ran the Tape Library at the Anglican Church, was a member of the Dutch Reformed Church but took her collection of tapes to St Mark's. Following a disagreement with the Vicar, she left St. Mark's taking her bookcase filled with tapes out of the vestry and to her home, so I continued to borrow tapes from her Home Library. I was going through a series by Malcolm Smith at that time, of Moses' leading the Children of Israel from slavery in Egypt into the Promised Land. I had just listened to one describing how God had told Moses to tell the Israelites to prepare to meet with God at the foot of Mount Sinai for God to instruct them of his commandments. There were ten of them.

The Israelites, in great expectation gathered at the foot of the mountain. When the lightning flashed, the thunder rolled and a thick cloud of smoke covered the mountain, God descended and spoke, giving them ten commandments. The Children of Israel trembled in fear and said to Moses, "You speak to us, and we will hear; but do not let God speak to us lest we die." Because the Israelites would rather listen to Moses than to God, they were given hundreds of commandments through the rest of Exodus, Leviticus, Numbers and Deuteronomy.

The teaching on that tape went on to say that many churchgoers are like that. They attend church but are not interested in a personal relationship with God for fear of God telling them what they don't want to hear. They go to church for then they are seen to be religious, but they are free to choose whether to listen.

I was upset when Sarah told me that she would be going away for a few months to visit family as I would not be able to get teaching tapes while she was away. I timidly offered to house the tape library while she was away and was thrilled when she said that it would be alright, but she would have to consult with

Tom, who managed the tape library with her. He would then bring it to me the following day. I took the next tape in the series to go on with while I waited.

The following day I experienced for the first time the harsh discipline of a loving Father God. This is how it happened: It was a glorious day. The sun shone brightly out of a clear blue sky, and I was excited as I impatiently awaited the delivery of the whole bookcase of tapes. An absolute banquet for my hungry soul to feast upon. Tom came, minus the bookcase. He announced that Sarah and he had discussed the tape library and it was decided that they could not let me have it while Sarah was away, but I could take a few tapes to go on with. My heart sank in disappointment. I would now not be able to satisfy my gluttony for knowledge.

There was a mighty clap of thunder and I jumped as I remembered the teaching of the tape that I had listened to the previous week. It related how, in John's Gospel, Jesus had spoken to the crowd telling them of his mission and death, calling on God to glorify his name, whereupon the voice of God responded saying, "I have glorified it and will glorify it again." The crowd standing by heard it and said, "It thundered!" while others said, "An angel spoke to him."

With the thunderclap that made me jump, Tom looked at my startled face and said, "It thundered!" No, I knew that it was God who had spoken, and He was angry!

"Wait," I said, and went into the lounge, took the tape that I had picked up the previous day, but I had not yet listened to it, and handed it to him saying, "That's fine Tom. I've finished with this one and I don't want any while Sarah is away."

I went into the bedroom, fell on my knees, and wept. I felt as though I was receiving a spiritual thrashing and knew that this time I certainly had 'asked for it'. (As a child I had often, with the words, *'You're asking for it,'* received a spanking from my mother when I had displeased her. I certainly could never remember 'asking for a spanking')!

With shame I confessed my pride, wanting to be admired for my superior knowledge while rejecting God's control in my life. From that day to this, I have never again listened to another teaching tape. I have been given tapes with the assurance that I would be blessed thereby. I have thanked the donor, taken the tape home, and returned it a week later with the words, "Thank you, so much, that was kind of you."

A few weeks later I went into the local bookshop to get a book that was recommended by the University. While searching for it another book kept 'flashing' at me. I ignored it as it was something I certainly did not want. The title was, 'Help Lord, the Devil Wants Me Fat'. I certainly do not want to have anything to do with the devil, so I continued to browse. Although the cover was not particularly striking or colourful it kept on 'flashing' at me. Eventually I thought 'I'll buy it and take it home and bin or burn it'.

I wondered why it had been so persistent in drawing my attention and was reminded of the several occasions that God had spoken to me through a scripture verse or phrase that seemed to persistently flash as though it was highlighted to draw my attention.

I sat down and began to read the opening chapter. It pointed out that the first temptation in the Bible was to tempt Eve to eat the forbidden fruit, and the first temptation of Jesus was to turn stones into bread. Jesus resisted, but Eve succumbed as did Adam to Eve's invitation to eat. There were several references to petitions to fast and the influence of fasting prayer. I found it gripping and read on. I strangely did not feel like any lunch that afternoon nor tea.

By evening I prepared a meal for the family but had a migraine, or sick headache so went to bed as I could not eat any dinner.

The next morning the headache had lifted, but I still had no appetite so continued to abstain. That was the beginning of what turned out to be a ten day fast. I was amazed to experience what the book described as the mind being enhanced through the shutting down of the digestive system. In that time, I could think more clearly, was greatly inspired, and had boundless energy. I could have gone on for longer, but after ten days of fasting, Karin became tearful and told me that I would die if I did not eat. As the book recommended an initial fast of ten days, I broke the fast.

I was disappointed that I had no spiritual encounters or visions during that time, but I did benefit by feeling extremely well. That evening I accepted an invitation from a neighbour, Anne, to come over as she and Neville were expecting a visit from a missionary from her church. The woman opened the meeting with prayer, and as she prayed, I felt my body growing bigger and heavier. 'What's going on?' I asked of the Lord in my own silent prayer. 'I've fasted for ten days, lost eight pounds in weight, so why am I feeling as though I'm getting so big and heavy?'

'You are a rock!' came the reply.

'No, Lord. You can't mean that. You called Peter a rock and said that on him you would build your church. You can't use me in building your church.' But as was His custom with me, he said no more.

* * *

*Let us draw near to God with a sincere heart
and with the full assurance of faith.*

(Hebrews 10:22)

Chapter 10
Mission Evolving

There followed many weeks of silence from God and emptiness in me. I no longer had clear direction. Had I offended God in some way? I did not know.

I was invited to a talk on 'Hearing God's Voice' at a Women's Auxiliary gathering. I had no desire to attend, but I went anyway.

The speaker started by asking the audience, "When did you last hear God speak to you?" Oh, I could answer that! Then she asked a second question, "Have you responded to what God was telling you?" I could answer that too; the answer was 'No.' There followed the message: "God is not going to speak to you again until you have obeyed His last directive."

I did not hear the rest of her talk for I knew what I must do. I went home and read the devotional reading for that morning, which was Matthew Chapter 28:16-20. Oh good; that was my favourite passage from the Bible, as it ended with Jesus' promise to me: "I'll be with you."

With a shock I noticed that the first part of verse 20 was suddenly illuminated: "*teaching them to obey everything that I have commanded you; a*nd surely I am with you always to the end of the age." I saw that the word 'and' tied the directive to the promise that Jesus had given me in my encounter with him at my conversion. With that, I realised that he was taking me a step further on my journey. That through teaching and preaching all that he commanded he would be with me. If I wanted to feel his presence and guidance, I would have to be obedient to that call.

Being a reserved person, I could not imagine that anyone would think that I was seriously considering preaching. This may have been funny if it was someone else challenging me to apply to be a preacher. I confess that I am sometimes cheeky when speaking to Jesus, but he doesn't seem to mind but understands that it is not meant with disrespect, but to be sure that I have heard correctly; so, my reply was, "OK Lord, then show me another woman in the pulpit."

I knew that I was safe there as I was not aware of any other women preachers in our District, and certainly none had preached in our church. The following Sunday I went into church and, looking at the notices that we were given to us on entering the church, I noticed that it was Local Preacher's Sunday, and the name of the visiting preacher was one I did not recognise. "Who is P Morgan?" I asked Ken, who was sitting along the pew. He shrugged, and replied, "I don't know the name. He's probably a new preacher in training."

Eventually the vestry door opened, and I gasped as a tubby little woman emerged from the vestry and climbed into the pulpit. "OK, Lord, very funny. I see her," I smiled. But my smile didn't last as she fumbled through the service, and I certainly was not impressed. "You see what I mean, Lord. She's dreadful. It's one of those occupations that is best left to men." Again, I had what I call a holy nudge, which conveyed to me that Jesus was not retracting his instruction. "OK, Lord, then let someone else say to me 'you should preach'." I knew that that would not happen among those here who knew me.

As we walked out of church Ken asked me, "What did you think of that?"

"Not much," was my reply.

"You could do better than that," he remarked. "Why don't you apply to preach?"

Well, there was my answer, so the following day I called on Fred, the Circuit Superintendent and told him that I wanted to preach. His reply was: "I don't believe that preaching is a role that women are called into, but because the Methodist Church welcomes not only women preachers, but also as ministers, I cannot refuse your request. I will put your name before the next Local Preacher's meeting, and we will take it from there."

"I agree with you." I said to Fred. "Give me a note to preach and we will either prove we're right or wrong," So I attended the next Local Preacher's meeting and was given a slot the following Sunday, to stand in for one of our 'on trial' Local Preachers who was unable to take his appointment. That service was scheduled as a trial service to be critiqued by Hillary, one of our senior LP's. Fred thought that it would be a good idea for me to be tested, probably 'found wanting'. I agreed for I did not mind if I failed. I knew that I, like Moses, did not have the 'gift of the gab'. (Here I am, Lord, send someone else.)

Having had no training, I prepared the service as best I could. I decided to use one of the Theology assignments for which I had received good marks. On Sunday morning I knew exactly how Jonah had felt when God had told him to go and preach to the people of Nineveh. I wanted to jump on the next ship to

Tarshish, but there was no escape now. The people of the Florida Methodist Church knew me as did Fred and the other ministers in that Circuit. So, like Esther I muttered, "OK, if I perish, I perish!"

Morning Worship began at 9h30 in the Florida Methodist Church. I followed the regular order of Service with the hymns and prayers and the set scripture readings, which I thought were far too truncated. The congregation needed to get the context, so instead of the ten verses dealing with Sacrificial giving, as prescribed in the Lectionary, I read the whole of two chapters, eighty-four verses of Exodus, describing the offerings to God in the Tabernacle in the Wilderness – first the washing bowl; then the altars; the sin offering; the burnt offering; the bread table; the lampstand; the altar of incense... I don't know if the congregation fell asleep sometime during the readings, but they were looking at me and appeared to be listening.

At last, I was able to deliver the sermon. I thought it went well. Being an introvert, I had feared that I would not manage to fill the hour. I glanced up at the clock on the back wall and saw that it was only 10h45. Worship services in my church started at 10h00 and finished around 11h00 which meant that I had only to fill another 15 minutes. That was good going for the only thing left was a hymn, prayers of intercession, the closing hymn and benediction. I announced the hymn and after the hymn the congregation remained standing, expecting the benediction, at last!

I suddenly realised that I had miscalculated my timing. This was not Horizon, but Florida Church. This was also a trial service so I couldn't leave out the prayers of Intercession. "Please be seated, we're not finished yet," I informed the congregation. Most of them sat obediently but several walked out.

The following day Fred called me to his office. "Hillary came over this morning to give me the report on your trail service," he announced.

"I know what you're going to say," I hung my head. "I forgot that I was in Florida not Horizon and got the timing wrong."

"Put a woman in the pulpit and she won't know when to stop chattering," he chuckled. "We'll forgive you that, *this time*, but you obviously don't know how to construct a sermon, among other things. I've asked Hillary to instruct you. She has agreed to be your mentor."

I was both relieved and surprised that Fred, of all people decided to keep me on. I met with Hillary, and she took me under her wing for the following year and taught me well until I was declared a fully-fledged Local Preacher.

Shortly after that our minister at Horizon left in the middle of that year, having been offered an appointment in America starting in September. The bishop sent us Ian, a young preacher who planned to candidate for the ministry. He had been working as youth pastor in one of the other churches in the district. Ian struggled to keep up with the pressure of preaching at both morning and evening services, doing pastoral visits and administration that was expected of him. He told me that he was going to give up his plans for the ministry and go back to secular employment and asked me to prepare a résumé for him.

In writing up his CV I realised that he was far better trained to being ordained as a Minister than he was qualified as a bookkeeper, which was his intention. "Oh, Lord," I muttered, "Can't Ian see that you have been preparing him for the ministry. Why doesn't he *listen* and respond to your call?"

"Why don't you!" came the voice in my head that I recognised at once.

I dropped my pen and began to laugh. "Oh, very funny," I chuckled. "O.K. I'll speak to Fred in the morning, and we can both have a laugh together." But it was not funny because an indescribable peace flooded over me. Jesus was indeed serious about it.

I went to see Fred the following morning and told him what had happened, but he did not take it seriously. "I accepted your request to be trained as a Local Preacher, even though I do not go along with the Methodist acceptance of women preachers, and there are a few women ministers, but they are all single. I certainly can't see a married woman being able to follow the disciplines of a minister. Wives of ministers often run the Women's Auxiliary, but we have no married women ministers. If your husband were a minister, you could run the WA. I could also approve of the wife serving as assistant pastor under him, though I don't know of any who do. I do not believe that God is calling you to ministry. It is not scriptural," he added. "Tell you husband to come and see me tomorrow and we'll talk about it."

Martin came with me the following evening to see Fred. After a long pep-talk Fred asked him how he felt about it. "I don't mind in the least if she goes into the ministry, nor do I mind moving about as ministers in the Methodist Church are expected to go where they are sent. I work from home, and I can do my job of property valuation wherever I am situated," was his reply. "So long as the church doesn't expect me run the Women's Auxiliary," he quipped, "or become involved in church work."

"Well, it's up to you. Go home and think about your role," replied Fred. "Then phone me when you are ready to accept the challenge, and I'll put her name forward."

I knew Martin, and that was never going to happen. We drove home in silence and went to bed that night, still in silence. There was nothing more to be said.

The next morning, I awoke while it was still dark. Martin always rose earlier than me and made tea for us after he dressed. I could hear him still in the shower. I thought about Fred's request and said, "Lord, it's up to you. If you want me in the ordained ministry, you will have to give Martin clarity on what he needs to do." With that the bedside light on Martin's side of the bed switched on by itself. "Fat lot of use that," I chuckled. "I have clarity. He's not here to see that," and I turned over and closed my eyes.

A few minutes later Martin came into the bedroom and began to dress. After a while he whispered, "Are you awake?"

"Mmm," I grunted.
"Did you switch the light on?"
"No," I said.
"WOW!" was his only comment. He continued dressing in silence, then left for work.

An hour later the phone rang, and it was Fred. He called to tell me that he had spoken with Martin and would be contacting the bishop to inform him that I was to candidate for the ordained ministry.

* * *

Jesus spoke ... saying,
"All authority has been given to me
in heaven and on earth.
Go therefore and make disciples of all nations,
baptizing them in the name of the Father and of the Son
and of the Holy Spirit,
and teaching them to obey everything
that I have commanded you.
And surely, I am with you always,
to the very end of the age."

(Matthew 28:20)

♫ ♫ ♫

1. I am Thine, O Lord, I have heard Thy voice,
    And it told Thy love to me;
    But I long to rise in the arms of faith
    And be closer drawn to Thee.

Draw me nearer, nearer blessed Lord,
To the cross where Thou hast died;
Draw me nearer, nearer, nearer blessed Lord,
To Thy precious, bleeding side.

2. Consecrate me now to Thy service, Lord,
    By the pow'r of grace divine;
    Let my soul look up with a steadfast hope,
    And my will be lost in Thine.

3. Oh, the pure delight of a single hour
    That before Thy throne I spend,
    When I kneel in prayer, and with Thee, my God,
    I commune as friend with friend!

4. There are depths of love that I cannot know
    Till I cross the narrow sea;
    There are heights of joy that I may not reach
    Till I rest in peace with Thee.

Fanny Crosby 1876

Chapter 11
Awakened Senses

Following my conversion, my senses had been stimulated by a spiritual awakening of the five human senses of sight, hearing, touch, smell, and taste. I cannot, nor should I call it a *sixth sense* as I was not given an additional sense, but those five human senses enhanced to see, hear, feel, smell what others have not been able to detect. I have not had my taste buds spiritually enhanced, even though Psalm 34:8 invites us to *'taste and see that the Lord is good'*.

Seeing into the Spirit Realm

The time that I am aware of seeing what was invisible to others was what I described in Chapter 3.

God was drawing me through visions, to creating in me a spiritual thirst. Seeing the halo of light around Joan Judd, and the beam of inspiration coming from God as she told of her experiences as a missionary enticed me.

The visible presence of the person sitting beside me in church that I describe in Chapter 4 I later realised was an angel sent to prepare me for my spiritual birth which followed a year later.

Seeing Jesus before me when I called on him to take my life was an unrepeatable vision which I will never forget. Seeing his beautiful face in my mind's-eye is ever before me as I pray.

I saw too, the spirit of my father at his funeral, but I will describe that in the next chapter.

Gardener or Guardian Angel

Another sight which I am convinced was an angel came to me as a gardener. Walking back from the corner shop one afternoon, an enormous Pit-bull Terrier charged out from the back gate of the house across the road from mine, and ran to me, snarling and salivating. I stopped in my tracks and turned towards him. As a child I had been bitten on the back of my leg by a dog and was told by those who know dogs, not to turn your back on a dog or run, nor to look into their eyes as that is seen by them to be challenging.

He stopped six feet from me, growling angrily. Avoiding eye contact but observing him with caution I took a wary step backwards. He leapt forward, now four feet away, teeth bared and snarling.

Every movement of mine brought on another angry growl and lurch of his body. Without moving my head, I glanced up the road but not a soul was in sight.

I dared not call out for that may further annoy the dog. Even if someone heard, would they respond? He wasn't budging and I dared not move. How long would I have to stand there in that quiet road? "Oh, Lord, I need your help. Please send an angel to my aid," I muttered.

A big black man appeared from the driveway of the house. He was dressed in a blue overall and sandals. Was he the gardener or a maintenance man – in sandals? His clothes were too clean for a workman at that time of the afternoon, and he held no tool in his hand, which I assume he would have had, had he been working, but he was a welcome sight.

He walked silently towards us. It was strange for such a heavily built man to tread so lightly as he walked on the gravel path making no sound at all. Nor did he call out to the dog, as I thought anyone would have done. He did not look at me, nor in any way even acknowledge my presence but with eyes fixed on the beast, he simply stopped behind the dog.

The dog immediately stopped growling, and without looking at the man, dropped his head, turned, and padded back through the open gate. The man turned and followed silently, closing the gate behind him, then up the gravel path and disappeared out of sight.

The man's actions and the dog's reaction puzzled me. It has had me wondering ever since. I asked the neighbour on the other side, and he said that he didn't know of any workman or gardener at that house then or around that time. Was it an angel? Are there black angels too, and dressed in blue overalls? I do not know.

There was no one there to tell me that they had not seen anyone. All that I know is that it was certainly an answer to prayer.

Companies of Angels

The angelic choir that I saw in my garden the evening of the visit by Jesus at my conversion, and the angels hovering above the Communion Table in the church that same evening at my reception into church membership was another vision that I will remember forever.

Seventeen years later I saw again many angels together with the spirits of departed relatives above the Communion Table at my pre-ordination service in Port Elizabeth.

Were my eyes open those evenings because those were turning points in my life, or are there always angels witnessing the sacrament of Holy Communion? Perhaps they are present at all services of worship and sacred moments.

Overshadowing Angels

One Good Friday morning as I was preaching, I had the feeling that someone was standing behind me in the pulpit, but of course, there was no one there. It was a comforting feeling however, as I was nervous about driving down to Natal after the service. There were always several fatal accidents on that road over the Easter weekend.

Emma, a member of my congregation in Malvern Church, later confirmed that on that morning she had seen someone standing over me and told me that she had often seen that figure behind me in the pulpit as I preached, or beside me at the Communion Table. When I asked her to describe the figure she said, "My eyesight is not so good anymore, so I can't describe him accurately, but he had either a high collar or something under his neck or chin."

I was showing Glynnis, a postcard that someone had sent me, that I thought particularly arresting, she exclaimed, "I saw that person standing behind you in the pulpit last Sunday, but then it disappeared so I thought that I must have imagined it," she said. It was a picture of 'St Mathew and the Angel', by Rembrandt.

"The angel?" I asked. "No, that man," she replied pointing at the man. I can't imagine that either one of the archangels or that St Matthew would come to watch

111

over me as I preached, but then, hadn't Jesus come to me at the turning point in my life? I am greatly humbled by the thought of the extent of the love of God and of the value he places on one of his children.

* * *

Do not forget to entertain strangers, for by so doing some have unwittingly entertained angels.
(Hebrews 13:2)

Hearing God speak through Scripture

I knew that the Bible was God's word to me, as a certain verse or passage would get my attention by flashing, as if in neon lights. One such life-changing event happened a few months after I had enrolled with a Bible College to do a full year Systematic Bible Study that took us, week by week through the whole Bible from Genesis through Revelation reading a book a week, followed by a lecture expounding that book in detail.

I had sat down to do my preparatory reading through the book of Isaiah. I was speed reading it when suddenly the second half of verse 9 in Chapter 41 flashed, as though in bright neon lights. *'You are my servant I have chosen you and not cast you off.'*

I stopped and read it again, but it was still highlighted. I went back and read the preceding verse and the next. "Lord, that's not a message for me but for Israel and Jacob," I said, but it flashed more strongly.

I read on and the next verse confirmed that it was for me as it was reinforced by the first part of verse 10, 'fear not for *I am with you,* be not dismayed, for I am your God.' These were the words that Jesus had spoken to me at my conversion.

I had wept, "What have I done, Lord? I thought that I was your precious *child*. Now you call me your *servant*!" but he did not enfold me in his loving embrace to comfort me. I read it again and there was no change. It still shone out like burnished bronze.

I reassured myself with the thought, 'Well, I suppose it's OK for wasn't Jesus the Servant of God?' I did not feel any consolation but continued with my reading. The purpose of that statement, that I was called to be God's servant, was revealed to me, and clarified seven years later at my call to ministry.

"All Scripture is God-breathed
and is useful for teaching, rebuking, correcting,
and training in righteousness,
so that the servant of God
may be thoroughly equipped for every good work"

(2 Timothy 3:16-17)

113

Silence can sometimes shout louder than words. Chapter 10 conveyed how God's silence hauled me to obedience to God's call.

God communicates through **Touch**

There have been times when I have had what I call a *holy hug*. It is the physical awareness of a loving embrace of God showing approval. It has come on a couple of occasions when I have been at a turning point when the only option was to do something that I feared might result in failure, the disapproval of others or be contrary to God's will. The 'holy hug' at those times was comforting and conveyed tenderness, saying: 'It's alright, my child, do it. I'm with you.'

There has also been the *nudge*, as a guiding force or prod to action. That has come when I was seeking to follow what I believe was God's directive that others perceived to be my will, contrary to Scripture, like the time when Fred said that it was not scriptural for women to preach or teach or speak in church. My response has always been, "Well then, Lord, if you want me to do it, make it happen," as God had done with Martin 'seeing the light'.

The *slap* or spiritual spanking I received on one occasion, when I turned away from listening to God and overindulged in teaching tapes so I would be admired for my superior spiritual knowledge. (This I suppose was like the sin of Eve & Adam.) I do not ever want a repeat of that.

Another touch of God is the *anointing*, or flow of blessing, as at my conversion in receiving God's Spirit. To expound on that sensation, I need to digress...

About a year after my dramatic conversion, I had been reading through Romans and came to chapter 6 with the reference to the significance of baptism. I thought that perhaps I needed to be baptised as it had meant nothing to me or little to my parents when I was an infant.

I phoned the leader of the Charismatic Fellowship that I and a couple of other Methodists attended on a Thursday night. I asked him about Believer's Baptism, and he told me that he occasionally baptised adults in his swimming pool but had not recently had any requests for baptism. He said that if any others requested it, he would let me know. The following day he phoned me saying, "You're not going to believe this, but after your phone call six others have independently contacted me or asked about baptism, so we will baptise you all next Thursday."

He then went on to tell me to read Romans 6, wear my swimsuit under a loose-fitting dress with coins in the hem to weigh it down, and bring dry clothing to change into after the baptism. I did all that and was disappointed that the sky did not open, nor did a voice of approval sound from the heavens. In fact, it was an unpleasant experience as the water prickled up my nose and stung for hours afterwards. At least, I had been obedient to what I thought was required of me.

Years later as I was preparing for ordination as a Methodist Minister, the Bishop asked me about my being rebaptised as an adult. I explained why I had requested it at the time. His reply was, that before my ordination I would have to come to terms with infant baptism, as the Methodist Church practiced it and could not condone any minister rebaptising adults later in life. I prayed about it and asked God to show me that infant baptism had God's blessing.

The following day I was surprised to get a call from one of my colleagues in the Circuit. "I have four families requesting baptism for their infants," he said. "I had planned to do that in two weeks' time, but with all the grand-parents, aunts, uncles and friends coming to the service, there won't be room for the regular congregation," he explained. "As you are down to preach here next Sunday, will you do two of the baptisms please? I've asked the parents and they are agreeable."

"Sure," I said, and then to God, "Thank you, Lord, I trust that you are going to show me that infant baptism has your blessing." I had not yet done a baptism, so I was anticipating enlightenment.

The two couples and the prospective godparents of the children came up to the font with their infants. I went through the preliminary procedure, and I took the first baby in my arms, baptising him in the name of the Father, and of the Son and of the Holy Spirit. God's blessing as a wave of warmth flowed tingling over me. I made to hand the child back to his waiting parents, but he turned away, muttering refusal, "uh-uh," and clung to me. So, I cuddled him for a while then tried again. This time he went, rather reluctantly. The second child I baptised with assurance.

After the service, as I stood at the door bidding farewell to the congregation as they left, the couple with the first baby asked me with mystified looks on their faces, "What did you do to Billy?"

"I baptised him, as you requested," was my reply.

"No, you must have done something special. He has never gone to a stranger and the fact that he not only went willingly when you took him, but that he didn't want to come back to us was astonishing," said his mother.

117

"He looked contented, more than that, *gratified*, in your arms," added his father.

"Ah! He felt it too," I replied. "God poured a blessing over us as I baptised him."

A few days later I received a call from Billy's mother to tell me that Billy had been an irritable baby from birth, but since his baptism he was an extremely happy child.

I have always known God's blessing to flow, guide and inspire me while conducting worship services.

A Driving Force

I was driving on the inside lane along a twisty, bendy stretch of the road down to Durban for our holiday in Shelly Beach. There was no hard shoulder on that stretch as the road curved around a rock faced hill. Clara and Karin were with me. All at once there was a sudden downpour as often happens at that time of the year. Rounding a bend in the road there was a car stopped by traffic cops at the side of the road in the lane ahead of me.

I glanced in my rear-view mirror and saw a stream of cars travelling at speed along the road to the right of me. None of them slowed down to let me into that lane. One of the traffic officers was standing to the rear of the car taking the registration number, the other traffic cop was standing in front of the car, straddling his motorcycle. Two small children were looking out of the back window with eyes like saucers, as I was speeding towards them. There was no way to avoid a tragic accident.

I slammed on the brakes, but the car kept going as it aquaplaned on the wet surface. The traffic officer standing at the rear of the car jumped aside and pressed against the side of the embankment. In desperation I cried out, "Lord help!"

Suddenly the steering wheel pulled firmly to the right. I gripped it tighter and tried to straighten it as the car was being forced to turn into the road and into the stream of fast-moving traffic. I could not straighten the wheel, as the force pulling it to the right was stronger than my efforts to correct it. The car brushed against the side of the passing truck, slowing my car to a stop, just six inches from the back of the car standing in my path.

The truck travelled on and the officer on the motorcycle chased after it. He returned a few minutes later and reported that the truck driver said that he felt no impact and would not be claiming damages, though his truck was dented. My car of course was badly scratched and buckled down the right side, but more importantly, no one was hurt.

What, or rather who, forced the steering wheel from my grip? I don't know. All that I can say is, "Thank you Lord for your answer to my cry for help."

* * *

You hem me in behind and before,
and you lay your hand upon me.
(Psalm 139:5)

God Communicates Through the Sense of **Smell**

I will describe two occasions of spiritually enhanced sense of smell in the next chapter.

Out of Body

Here I am at age eighty-two, coming to the end of this book, and probably nearing the end of my life on earth. So, I share with you what may have been my only out-of-body experience... or it may have been simply a confused, half-asleep impression.

At 4.00am I got up to go to the toilet but in the doorway, I turned and saw that I was still lying in my bed, so I went back into my body and slumbered on.

At around 6.00am I awoke again with a start, as I had the sensation of someone sticking a finger or hand down my throat. I sat up and cried out, "Get off!" Then saw that there was nothing or no one there. I turned and saw myself still lying peacefully. I got up and went

120

to the toilet but still felt detached. I wondered if I was going du-lally or experiencing the onset of Alzheimer's or senile dementia. Would I begin wandering up and down the passage or get disorientated? I went back to bed and into my body and dozed off again.

At 7.15am I awoke feeling well-rested and back to my normal self again. What was that all about? All part of the strange experiences of life.

* * *

Therefore, since we are surrounded
by such a great cloud of witnesses,
let us throw off everything that hinders
and the sin that so easily entangles.
And let us run with perseverance
the race marked out for us.

(Hebrews 12:1)

Chapter 12
Heaven's Portal

Standing at Heaven's Gates

Shortly after my ordination a member of my congregation asked me, "As a woman minister how do you cope with conducting funerals? Isn't that side of your work awfully depressing and stressful?"

"Just the opposite," I said. "I am tremendously blessed and edified while I am conducting the funeral, being aware that I'm standing on the brink of eternity with one foot in this world, ministering to the bereaved, and the other foot in heaven. I have a clear sense of the spiritual presence of the deceased observing his or her relatives and friends gathered there grieving and bidding them farewell, and those on the other side joyfully welcoming them."

The Funeral Wake Reflects the Heavenly Reunion

After the funeral of one of our uncles my brother remarked, "I can't understand that people attend funerals looking sad, weeping through the service, then go into the hall for refreshments, chatting and laughing together with family and friends."

My reply was, "At the gathering after the service, what's happening on earth is simply a reflection of what's going on in heaven. It's a happy reunion with family and friends who have been out of touch for a long time."

Dad's Funeral

While waiting at the airport to board the plane for my flight to Amanzimtoti where my mother and father had a retirement home, I'd been reading a book. I then looked up at the clock to see how much longer to my flight's departure. My thoughts turned to my parents. My Mom had phoned early that morning to tell me that Dad had suffered another heart attack and been taken by ambulance to the hospital in Durban. She sounded distressed so I told her that I would get the next flight to be with her and to see him. The clock on the wall showed ten minutes to twelve – almost an hour to the flight.

My thoughts turned to my father. It was ten years since his first attack. The doctor had told him then that he could last another ten years if he stopped smoking, watched his diet, and exercised daily. He had faithfully done all that. Was this now the beginning of the end? Was he going to die? Was he saved? I wasn't sure and prayed, "Lord, please don't take him just yet.

Let me get there in time to see him, giving me the opportunity to pray with him and lead him to a commitment and salvation. Amen"

I heard the words, *'In my Father's house are many mansions... I have a place prepared for him.'* I breathed a "Thank you, Lord." With the assurance that I would indeed see him and have the joy of leading him to make a commitment to receive entry into heaven. Thus comforted I settled to reading again.

After my conversion I had hoped for a visit from my parents so that I could lead them to Christ, but I had not seen them again. I was delighted that I would now have that opportunity to witness to them, for Jesus had assured me that I would have my request, so I settled down to read and wait for the signal to board the plane.

Just over an hour later, my brother Junior met me at the airport. As I got into the car I asked him, "Is Mum at the hospital or at home?"

"She's at the flat and Clara is there too," was his reply.

"Are we going to pick her up or shall we go to the hospital to see Dad first?" I asked.

There was a long pause before he replied, "Dad passed away at ten to twelve."

My heart sank. Jesus had promised that I would see him and lead him to commitment before he died! But had he? No, he had not. I realised what he had said was, *'In my Father's house are many mansions, I have a place prepared for him.'* Well, it was alright then. Didn't the scriptures go on to say: 'I will take you to be with me that where I am you may be also''?

Three days later, at my father's funeral I was sitting in the front pew between my mother and sister Clara, facing the coffin. The service had not yet begun, and my mother was sobbing quietly. All at once my father appeared standing with his back to us, looking at the coffin. I was surprised and disappointed that he ignored us and was not interested in who was there to mourn him. Why was Dad ignoring us, especially Mum? Why was he not reaching out to comfort her?

Those years in retirement with all the children out of the house, especially during the past ten years and being a meticulous man, he had set his mind to make the most of the time by being a loving and attentive husband, going out of his way to minister to his wife and sensitive to her every need and want.

But there he stood gazing at his coffin, ignoring Mum and the rest of us. I heard his thoughts - telepathically, "So this is my funeral and there are my earthly remains, an empty shell, no longer needed. I am here now."

Behind him, further back and on a slightly higher level, I sensed and heard his departed relatives, though I did not see them. They were calling to him to come back to the reunion celebration. They called to him in Holland's, his mother tongue, "Adriaan, wat doet ye nou? Kom ye dan terug," (Adrian, what are you doing? Come back here.) They too appeared to be oblivious of the family and friends gathered at his funeral, and of the coffin which was Dad's centre of attention. Then Dad replied, also in High Dutch, 'Ja, ik kom.' (Yes, I'm coming.)

As I watched my father and listened to the jollifications of his welcome party I wondered: 'So where is Jesus?'

On later reflection, I realised that Jesus had spoiled every funeral that he had attended by raising the body; so that was why he was not there! Jesus is among the living not the dead – in heaven and on earth.

Jonathan's Funeral

It was the last day of Jonathan's military service training. I was waiting for the phone call from him, asking me to come and pick him up at the regular drop-off point. The phone rang and it was not Jon, but Martin. He was choking with emotion as he announced, "Terrible news!"

"What is it?" I asked, realising that it was indeed dreadful to affect him thus.

"Jon's been killed in a car accident," he replied. "There are three army officers here at the house now. They came with the news."

"I'm coming home," I said, and rang off. On my way home the thoughts whirled around in my head: 'It can't be true… They must have made a mistake… Not my child… It must have been someone else's child… He's only nineteen,' then: 'of course it can be true… Children die… why should it be someone else's child? I can cope with it better than many other parents.'

In that half-hour's drive home, I went through the whole grieving process of disbelief, denial, blaming, bargaining, anger, guilt, depression, despair, and then through prayer to acceptance, and even thanksgiving.

Jon's in a wonderful place. We don't understand why, but God is always worthy of praise. He can use adversity for our growth and his glory. He is the resurrection and the life.

In planning and preparing for Jon's funeral we were all aware that he was there with us telling us what hymns he wanted. They were not the usual funeral hymns, but they were his choice – his favourite hymn as a child: *'Low in the grave he lay, Jesus my Saviour... Up from the grave he arose, a mighty triumph o'er his foes.'* and *'There's a light upon the mountains...'*

A week after his funeral, while introducing myself to a prospective new member, she asked me, "How many children do you have?" I hesitated for the briefest of moments, for it would not be appropriate to tell her of our recent bereavement and realising too that I could not deny the existence of Jonathan, for after all, he was still alive, and more so than before, I replied, "Three," and felt a warmth flowing over my soul. Yes, Jonathan is still my child though no longer with us.

A year before his death I had done an exercise with the youth group at the church. They were to lie perfectly relaxed on the floor with their eyes closed and to imagine that they were a plant growing in the ground... I then ask them to feel their roots and the soil in which they were growing... After a while I asked them to note their stems, branches, leaves, buds, blooms, and fruit, if there were any, and to see if there were insects around them... then to see the gardener come along and to notice what he did... When they were ready, to open their eyes.

When every eye was open, I asked them to sit up and listen to the reading of the Vine and Gardener in John 15:1-11 and think about the shrub that they had imagined and to relate it to the scripture lesson.

Jon told me that he saw himself as a rather scraggy rosebush. The gardener then came and tenderly pruned the bush which then produced a mass of fragrant white blooms. The gardener picked the best blooms and took them home in his arms.

When we laid Jon's ashes in the Garden of Remembrance, we planted a white rosebush over them. Three months later the three-foot-tall rosebush was covered in thirty-six magnificent, perfectly formed and heavily fragranced blooms. Visitors to the garden commented on the rosebush, saying that they had never seen anything like it before.

On several occasions, in the years that followed, I often sensed Jon's presence in the room. Without telling the others about it, Karin also remarked on his presence, though at the time we had not been talking about him.

Through having obtained a Bachelor of Theology degree, and being a mature-age candidate, my years of probation had been reduced from the regulation six years to four years. Because of this at my pre-ordination service of reception into full connection I was not accompanied by the ordinands that I had travelled with in training. The service was in Port Elizabeth so family and friends from Johannesburg had not travelled down to be with me. I was the only ordinand who was not accompanied by family or friends.

It happened to be on the day of Jon's 21st Birthday and sitting on my own I was thinking that if Jon were still with us, I would have asked for a deferment of my ordination, so that I could be at home to celebrate his 21st birthday.

All at once I heard Jon's cheerful voice saying, "You're not alone Mum, I'm here, and many others. See them and the crowd of angels above the Communion Table." Yes, I did see them, and my heart rejoiced at being given the vision.

Martin's Visit

I chaired a Church Council meeting where the treasurer gave me a lot of flak. I am usually slow to counter-attack or defend my position, but this time I had been quick to justify the decision and gained the support of the other members. Gavin was thus humiliated and silenced.

When I got home after the meeting, I went into the house unlocking and relocking the door behind me. All at once I sensed Martins' presence and there was the strong smell of pine in the room. I heard Martin's voice, "I'm so proud of you." I was startled and looked around me to see if there was anything giving off a pine odour, but there was nothing.

Martin had died unexpectedly in a pine forest a few months earlier, and now came to commend me.

Julie's, Margaret's and Emma's Visions

While on pastoral visits I have often been told about spirit visitors or visions of angels. Julie told me of sitting at her sister's bedside and seeing the most beautiful angel standing in the corner of the room. "He was magnificent, about seven foot tall," she said. "He wore a beautifully embroidered waistcoat encrusted with sparkling gemstones and jewels. He knew that I had seen him and raised a finger to his lips warning me to say nothing of his presence. He remained standing there all afternoon. Later I needed to go to the bathroom and when I got back my sister had passed on and the angel too was no longer there," she told me. "He must have come to fetch her. I hope that when I go, he comes to fetch me. I'd love to see him again," she added.

A year later she too died, but I was not at her bedside at the time, and if I had, there is no reason why I should have seen anything. I do hope that she got her wish, and I can think of no reason why she would not.

Margaret went into hospital and her husband told me after coming home from visiting her that she had asked him, "Who are all these people standing around in this ward?" He was puzzled as she was in a private ward, and he said that he was her only visitor then. I did not say anything as she was not terminally ill, but I thought, 'Oh dear, she's on her way out,' as I have so often heard of people having a vision of relatives coming to escort them to the hereafter. The following morning Bill phoned me to tell me that Margaret had died in the night.

Emma, the person at Malvern Methodist Church who, on several occasions, saw an angel or spirit standing behind me as I conducted worship, also told me that she often saw the ghost of a man coming into the church and sitting in the front pew. She told me then that she had been born with a caul, or the amniotic sack over her face, so she had extra sensory perception and often saw spirits and angels.

A week after her husband died, she told me that she had been sorting through his papers but couldn't find the one relating to his insurance policy. That night he stood beside her bed and said, "Don't distress yourself, darling. Look in the back of the book that I was reading when I had the heart attack and was taken into hospital. I had been going through those papers and slipped them into the back of the book. In tidying away, you put the book in the bookcase. It's there." The next morning, she found the papers where he had put them.

Eric's Experiences

My husband Eric had been busy all week with physically challenging construction digging an enormous pond in the garden and laying a path down from the decking to the edge of the pond. That evening he told me that while he was laying the heavy stone slabs for the path, he saw several people standing around in the garden, and his late wife, Muriel, was among them. He thought that they were inviting him to join them, but he was too busy and wanted to get on with laying the path. He was seventy-nine at the time, and remembering

Bill's account of Margaret's vision, I thought, 'Oh no, he's being fetched and will soon go.'

The following morning, he brought me a cup of tea in bed. He was laughing as he told me, "A funny thing happened. I filled the kettle and switched it on to boil. Next thing I woke up and found myself lying curled up on the floor as though I had been sleeping there, so I got up and made the tea." This, I though, confirmed my fears - his time was up.

A few months later, on the day of his eightieth birthday Eric was relaxing in his recliner with eyes closed. I thought that he was sleeping, but then he said, "Thank you!"

"What was that about?" I asked.

"Muriel is here," he said. "I smell her perfume; lily-of-the-valley." He said no more but lay back smiling contentedly. I did not smell, see, or sense anything, but it was a wonderful birthday blessing for him.

He's now ninety-two and still with me, active and as energetic as ever. Ah well, he 'missed the boat' twelve years ago, and I'm pleased to note, in spite of the invitation to join Muriel and friends, he chose to stay with me, for better or for worse.

Pets' afterlife and Psychic Sense

One night, shortly after I had settled into bed, I sensed my cat who had died two days before, jumping in through the window, as she always did, and leaping onto the foot of my bed where she slept.

It is a pity that animals cannot speak, but they certainly have no difficulty in communicating their wants, needs and frame of mind. One evening, Bushski, our Siamese cat who had been lying curled up on the chair across the room from me, suddenly sat up and turned to look intently at the doorway. She sat like that for about five to ten minutes staring fixedly at whatever was there. I could not see anything, but she was extremely alert and responsive to whoever was there communicating with her.

My sister Betty, a cat lover, had died the week before and I felt sure that it was she, come to tell me that heaven is all that I had said it was, or not at all like that. Ah well, now she knew and had come to share the news with me, but I unfortunately could neither see nor hear her; but Bushski certainly could.

I sensed the communication going on between the two of them. Then after about five to ten minutes of this interaction, Bushski gave a meow and nod as if in response to whatever Betty had said and turned to settled down again as the aura turned from the doorway and left.

* * *

The Covenant Prayer

(This is a 17th Century Covenant Prayer adapted by John Wesley, used annually by the Methodist Church, and adopted by many other denominations)

"I am no longer my own, but Yours.
Put me to what You will, rank me with whom You will;
Put me to doing, put me to suffering;
Let me be employed for You or laid aside for You,
Exalted for You, or brought low for You;
Let me be full, let me be empty;
Let me have all things, let me have nothing:
I freely and wholeheartedly
yield all things to Your pleasure and disposal.

And now, glorious, and blessed GOD,
Father, Son and Holy Spirit,
You are mine and I am Yours.

So be it.

And the covenant now made on earth,
Let it be ratified in heaven.

Amen."

Dear Reader,

I pray that you have been blessed and inspired
in reading this book.

We are all unique individuals; no two people
have the same experience of a relationship with God.

God knows each of us intimately,
understands our frailties, loves us
and wants us to experience fullness of life in Him.

Some assume that He is a wrathful God, but it is only
things that rebel against experiencing God's love that He
can't bear and rebukes.

Joan can be contact at: joan.lougheed@btinternet.com

Printed in Great Britain
by Amazon